THE SECULARIZATION OF MODERN CULTURES

The Secularization
of Modern Cultures

BERNARD EUGENE MELAND

NEW YORK
OXFORD UNIVERSITY PRESS
1966

TO UNFORGETTABLE DAYS IN INDIA
AND TO THE MEMORY OF ONE
WHO SHARED THEM WITH ME

Foreword

When I was given the opportunity to return to India to give the Barrows Lectures a second time, I had no hesitancy about choosing the subject of my lectures. During my visit to India in 1957-58 the one firm impression that fixed in my mind was that secularization was proceeding at a rapid pace, affecting not only the internal affairs of the nation, but also the image of Indian culture that was being projected abroad. My long concern with the history of liberalism in modern Europe and America had already alerted me to secularizing tendencies in the West. I was aware, too, that, from the turn of the century on, India's intellectual leaders had been in touch with these developments in the West and, to some extent, had influenced Indian thinking in that direction. With the coming of independence in 1947, a new and concerted effort was initiated, largely under the influence and leadership of India's first Prime Minister, Jawaharlal Nehru, to rally the cultural forces of the new nation around the ideal of a secular state, and to bring the full force of India's own character and heritage to this experiment in secularization. Since the close of World War II political and cul-

tural revolutions have taken place in practically every nation around the globe, and secularization, as a radical departure from historic guidelines and sensibilities, has clearly
emerged as one of the significant tendencies of modern
times. Today it is occurring on a scale that is probably without precedent in the history of civilization. Therefore, in
undertaking to give the Barrows Lectures for 1964-65, I de-
cided to address myself to secularization as a world phenomenon, giving special attention to the two areas with which I
had had direct acquaintance: Western culture and modern
India.

As I discussed the problem of secularization with various
people in India it became evident that I had focused upon
an area of issues that was alive and insistent to many modern
Indians who were concerned with the nation's present cultural changes. My intention in these lectures has been to
embrace the full scope of secularizing tendencies, trying
first to understand the phenomenon of secularization as it
is occurring in present-day societies, and then to assess some
of its implications. Ultimately I have been concerned to ask,
What do these secularizing tendencies indicate about the
status and significance of religious sensibilities in present-day
cultures, where science and technology are coming into
ascendancy, and where historical institutions, with their
legacies of restraint and sensibilities, appear to be on the
wane?

India in this respect is a window to the world among
modern nations that are struggling to achieve their identity
and to find their present role in the affairs of the world. The
processes at work in Indian society parallel many of those
of other younger nations, though the circumstances in some
instances obviously differ radically. For one thing, India's
fight to become a modern nation was a prolonged struggle
at the parliamentary level before it became a traumatic so-

cial crisis attended by outbursts of violence and tragedy. In contrast to the social and political upheavals in other Asian countries, such as Indonesia or even China, and Middle Eastern countries, such as those of Africa, India's process of change has been more evolutionary than revolutionary. The interim of revolt initiated by Mahatma Gandhi and the younger Nehru in the years preceding 1947 was so dramatic in its impact that it appeared more revolutionary and innovating than it actually was in the context of the nation's history from the late nineteenth century onward. It has been argued that the insistent and persistent measures urged by these Indian leaders hastened and precipitated, in climactic decisions, what had been subtly evolving in India since the organization of the Indian Congress in 1885. This fact, that sustaining overtones of evolving parliamentary practices accompanied, and lay back of, more revolutionary and innovating forces of Indian social reform, gave to this spearhead of revolt a considerable background of cultural resources, even as it served to censor and often to suppress its innovating efforts. Even in the men who led the revolt, notably Gandhi and Nehru, this background of inherited cultural resources spoke insistently and eloquently. India thus came into its modern status as an independent nation without breaking radically with its past or with structures of government that had carried the memories and policies of that past into its present deliberations and decisions.

Secularization in India, therefore, while certainly present and steadily advancing, is not the catastrophic or disruptive force it has proven to be in other modern cultures where changes have been precipitous, enacted almost by fiat by one political faction or another in the seizure of power. In a way this detracts from the excitement and drama of its cultural change, but, on the other hand, it provides a more orderly canvass of events on which we may observe what is present or implicit in the secularizing currents that are now changing the character of modern societies throughout the world.

When I had finished delivering these lectures at Poona, several Indian scholars in my audience urged that I have the lectures published in India so that the form of addressing the Indian people might be retained. They felt that the force of what was being said could best be conveyed by holding to this direct manner of speaking. The editors of Oxford University Press, taking this concern into account, have kindly agreed to publish the lectures in this form. The book thus becomes a dialogue between American and Indian thinking upon a common problem, and thus one which I would hope American as well as Indian readers might find of interest.

Chicago, Illinois   B.E.M.
June 1965

Acknowledgments

The indebtedness I have incurred in presenting these lectures extends to many people and places. I am grateful first of all to Dr. Jerald C. Brauer, Dean of the Divinity School, and to The Committee on The Haskell and Barrows Lectureships of the University of Chicago for appointing me to the Barrows Lectureship for 1964-65. I am also grateful to Dr. Edward H. Levi, Provost of the University of Chicago, for making the arrangements with the administrative officers of the University of Calcutta and the University of Poona for the presentation of the lectures at these two universities. I wish to express my appreciation to Vice Chancellor Malik and Dr. G. C. Raychaudhuri, Registrar, of the University of Calcutta, as well as to various faculty members of that University, for their courtesies and co-operation during the presentation of the lectures in Calcutta. I wish also to express my appreciation to Dr. N. V. Gadgil, Vice Chancellor of the University of Poona, and to Professor Datto Vaman Potdar, former Vice Chancellor, through whom earlier arrangements for the lectures were made, for their courtesies during my visit to Poona, as well as to Mr. G. M. Watve of the Registrar's Office for his constant attention to my needs throughout that period. I am particularly indebted to The American Institute for Indian Studies in Poona and to its directors, Dr. McCrea Hazlett and Dr. Richard Lambert, for their kindness in providing hospitality for Mrs. Meland and me in the Institute's hostel, for rewarding associations with visiting scholars of the Institute, and for their support of my efforts.

I am also individually indebted to a number of people who, in various ways, contributed to making our visit in India profitable and enjoyable, particularly Dr. and Mrs. Malcolm Willey of the Ford Foundation in Calcutta, Professor N. V. Banarjee and Dr. S. S. Barlingay of the Department of Philosophy in the University of New Delhi, and their colleagues, Dr. James Swamidasan of the Philosophy Department in Elphinstone College, Bombay University, Mr. and Mrs. Jack McCray and Karen McCray and the Rev. Mr. Gaston Singh of Bombay, and Mrs. Ketkar, Warden of the Hostel at the American Institute of Indian Studies. I wish to make special mention of my gratitude to Dr. Charles White of the University of Pennsylvania and Dr. J. A. B. Van Buitenen of the University of Chicago, who were then visiting scholars of the Institute in Poona, whose helpfulness to Mrs. Meland and me meant more than they could realize.

I wish also to acknowledge my indebtedness to the following publishers, for permission to quote from works published by them:

Council on Foreign Relations, and Harper and Row; Dhoomi Mal Ram Chand, New Delhi; Oxford University Press, New York; Princeton University Press; Universal Book and Stationery Co., Delhi; University of Chicago Press; D. Van Nostrand Company, Princeton, N.J.; Sahitya Akademi, New Delhi; the editors of *Foreign Affairs*, New York; and the editors of *Religion and Society*, published by The Christian Institute for the Study of Religion and Society, Bangalore, India.

Contents

Sources of Secularization

The general theme with which we shall be occupied through-out these six lectures is the secularization of modern cultures. In order that we may have at least a preliminary idea of what we shall be discussing, let me indicate at the outset what it is we are pointing to in a society when we speak of secularization. Simply stated, and in its barest terms, secularization is the movement away from traditionally accepted norms and sensibilities in the life interests and habits of a people—a departure from an historical order of life that presupposes religious sanctions. More often the word "secular" is simply contrasted with "religious" or "sacred." The reason for this contrast is that cultures have generally conceived of themselves as having arisen from religious origins, and to be responsive to an order of existence which is consonant with such origins. Changes have continually occurred within these societies, but however much this historical order of life may have changed through reforms or retrogression, the presuppositions of its life have remained intact. Today, in one modern society after another, this inherited basis of meaning and value is being dissolved, rejected, or ignored. And in some instances it is being replaced by a new shape of thought and by a new ethos.

Secularization looms upon the horizon of every culture of our time wherever there are aspirations to become modern and in tune with the events of present history. This is a situation that is at once ominous and yet full of promise. It is ominous because of what it presupposes with regard to past history and its sensibilities, what it is ready to relinquish; it is full of promise because of its courage and audacity in the use of present facilities, ideas, and aspirations.

Secularization today arises from many sources and influences, and it takes a variety of forms. It is hardly pertinent therefore to say one is *for* or *against* secularization until one has clarified the term within a given context. And even then, if one is discriminating in his judgments, he may find that it is not a matter that he can categorically approve or disapprove, but a situation in which he must move selectively and judiciously in dealing both with what is offered and with what is denied.

It is not my intention to assume a partisan view on this problem, though, no doubt, my predilections and preferences are bound to show through; rather it is my concern to look with candor at the various aspects of this phenomenon of secularization in our time, and to consider the implications for modern cultures and for our humanity which appear to arise from them.

Let us look at the problem of secularization as a whole, noting the various ways in which this term "secular" is being understood and the many sources from which the process itself proceeds. In talking with some of your Indian scholars and leaders, I have found that the term "secular" takes on various shades of meaning in your country, depending upon the kind of group with whom one is speaking. Among the Hindu philosophers who identify themselves with modern Hinduism, the movement that is commonly referred to as "Neo-Hinduism," secularism has come to have the specific meaning of directing the spiritual vision of man to "purposive action in present history." This, no doubt, represents an effort to counteract the meaning of the spiritual life commonly ascribed to the doctrine of *Maya*, in which the world of common affairs was regarded as illusion. In a spirited statement, voicing the new meaning of the Hindu faith, your President, Dr. Radhakrishnan, wrote,

The world is not an illusion; it is not nothingness, for it is willed by God and therefore is real. Its total reality is radically different from the being of absolute God. Absolute alone has non-created divine reality; all else is dependent, created reality. This is the significance of the doctrine of *Maya*. It does not mean that the temporal process is a tragedy or an aberration. The reality of the world is not in itself but it is in the thought and being of the Creator. It is what God thought and willed it to be before it was.[1]

Here secularism tends not to be dissociated from the Hindu faith, or even to be rebellious toward its tradition. Rather, it is understood, much as religious liberalism in the West has been understood, as a movement within the faith to bring the religious heritage of the culture to bear directly upon this world and its affairs. It involves a certain transmutation of ideas and religious affirmations, but not their rejection. Thus, in speaking of the secular government of India in the foreword to a work on *The National Culture of India*, Dr. Radhakrishnan was led to write, "Secularism here does not mean irreligion or atheism, or even stress on material comforts. It proclaims that it lays stress on the universality of spiritual values which may be attained by a variety of ways."[2]

[1] Paul Schilpp (ed.), *The Philosophy of Sarvepalli Radhakrishnan*, New York: Tudor, 1952, p. 41.
[2] S. Abid Husain, *The National Culture of India*, Bombay: Jaico Publishing House, 1955, pp. vii-viii.

This general Neo-Hindu view of secularism, relating the religious vision to the practical affairs of society, was stated more concretely by Mahatma Gandhi during the later stage of his thought. He was aware of the new secular vision awakening in India, and saw in it the "religious dynamic" for building the new national life that was then emerging. Said Mahatma Gandhi,

Man's ultimate aim is the realization of God, and all his activities, social, political, religious, have to be guided by the ultimate aim of the vision of God. The immediate service of all human beings becomes a necessary part of the endeavor, simply because the only way to find out God is to see Him in His creation and be one with it. This can only be done by service of all. I am a part and parcel of the whole, and I cannot find Him apart from the rest of humanity. My countrymen are my nearest neighbors. They have become so helpless, so resourceless, so inert that I must concentrate myself on serving them. If I could persuade myself that I should find Him in a Himalayan cave I would proceed there immediately. But I know that I can not find Him apart from humanity.[3]

This, then, is one way in which secularism is being understood in this country. There is a second way: among creative writers and artists in India, secularism takes on a more explicit iconoclastic note.[4] While something of this Neo-Hindu view is retained, these people of literature and modern art seem more conscious of the fact that they are letting go of something basic in Indian tradition, that they are relinquishing philosophical concepts and premises as well as

---

[3] *Harijan*, August 29, 1936. Quoted in P. D. Devanandan, "Contemporary Hindu Secularism," *Religion and Society*, IX, 1 (March 1962), 29.
[4] Evidence of a secularizing mood in the art and literature of modern India is to be found in various centers, particularly in northern India. A glimpse of some of these tendencies is given in *Modern Trends in Indian Painting* by Manohar Kaul, New Delhi: Dhoomimal Ramchand, 1961, and in *Contemporary Indian Literature*, A Symposium, New Delhi: Sahitya Akademi, 1957. The chapter by S. H. Vatsyayan on Hindi Literature is particularly illuminating. See also articles in *Orient Review*.

mythological and mystical notions which in the past have given a transcendent orientation to the human scene. In its place they are substituting something quite mundane, namely, the analysis of man in his everyday existence. The resources for this task are more apt to be drawn from the current cultural disciplines such as the physical sciences, modern psychology, psychoanalysis, anthropology, and other social sciences. And when they use the term secular in this context, it is apt to imply something more than an ideological departure from tradition. It implies cultural freedom from the oppressive restraints of established religions, providing some measure of detachment, and thereby enabling discerning people of your culture to assume a critical stance in relation to traditional mores or customs. Among certain groups, this very detachment has resulted in social criticism and efforts toward social change. It may be argued that this corporate critical attitude has been an important factor in bringing about recent social reforms on a national scale and in opening the way for a more inclusive, cosmopolitan culture, which is sometimes referred to as a "third culture" in India.

Among a third group of your citizens, the word "secularism" takes on an ominous import, as meaning a departure from familiar ways, resulting from the emphasis upon science in the schools and from the impact of industrialization on family, village, and city life in India. This turn of mind appears more frequently among devout Hindus who take the communal pattern of their faith quite seriously, and who see this filial pattern of existence definitely under threat in what is presently occurring.

When I reported upon this view of secularism to a group of philosophers in New Delhi, elaborating a bit more on the present nature of this concern, they found it hard to believe that any discerning Indian would put forth this kind of view. They were sure that it was wholly unrepresentative of any informed Indian opinion, and if held, it expressed the view of a very small minority of Hindus.

On this point, I cannot give a firm judgment. All I can say is that it concerned one Vice Chancellor in a major university very much, as it did a historian in one of the colleges in north India. And these men didn't think they were speaking solely for themselves. They spoke as if they were interpreting the beliefs of a sizable number of the Hindu community. My reason for assuming that they may be correct is that it expresses quite a familiar reaction to these *acids of modernity* in other cultures, notably in the United States.

What one must understand, I think, is that philosophers who represent the Neo-Hindu movement tend to assume that if an idea identified as "secular" can be assimilated to the general philosophical outlook with which traditional values are expressed, no serious negation has occurred. However, one for whom the piety of faith looms large will be keenly sensitive to breaches in the feeling-tone that are brought about by social changes as they affect historical sensibilities.

Since I shall be using the term "sensibilities" frequently in these lectures to express what is being transformed or lost to modern cultures as a result of secularization, let me pause a moment to indicate what I mean to convey by it. The word "sensibility" is commonly defined as "a capacity to respond to esthetic and emotional stimuli," and therefore is understood rather restrictively to apply to people of a particularly sensitive nature, or to people trained to be discriminating in their tastes. The words "taste" and "style" have more commonly been pre-empted by the arts. My own approach to human living and to the life of any culture presupposes that these terms apply more generally to the whole range of responses expressive of the human spirit. Taste and style enter into matters of moral behavior and religion, philosophical reflection or inquiry, and social action, as well as the arts. Thus I use the word "sensibilities" in a wider sense to convey a capacity in all human beings to respond appreciatively and with restraint to accepted ways of feeling or behavior within any culture, either as a consequence of concurring with the human values implied, or out of respect or consideration for the corporate concerns of the community. There are other words more commonly used in social science literature to connote something of this meaning, words such as "ethos," "mores," "custom," or "tradition." These terms are useful for designating the over-all trends of accepted attitudes and behavior; but they do not do justice to the diversity of responses that occur within these general trends, nor to the sensitivities involved in these variations within a common ethos. Thus they invariably overstate or blur the implications of the social consensus.

Sensibility as I use the term, however, implies something more than an extension of the appreciative dimension to common experiences. It presupposes a way of understanding man and the human mind. It partakes of the organismic view that sees the sensible and rational powers of man suffused and interrelated. "We think with our bodies," said Whitehead. Thinking, in other words, is a holistic occurrence that presupposes bodily relations and responses which are integral to the act of cognition, though distinguishable from it. Sensibilities are thus the carriers of nascent and incipient acts of rational judgment or decision, and can be considered the persisting, durable source or structure of human perception and feeling from which overt acts erupt into conscious behavior. Conscious acts, however, often over-act. That is, the mind's explicit formulation of an idea or an assertion tends to over-state, or to state too sharply, the intention initially awakened in sensibilities. For this reason the overt, radical rejection of historical notions or values expressed through verbalization may appear more iconoclastic and negative than it actually is to the individual's total psychical self. Thus something of what appears rejected or relinquished persists in the person even as he disavows identification with it. This observation will help to explain why historical sensibilities tend to persist as a motivating or inhibiting force among certain people of a culture even when they become openly critical of customs and traditions. Consciously they may speak out against these social controls; but perceptually, emotionally, psychically, they may still share in the feeling-tone of such inherited controls, even while voicing their protests. Hence liberals and modernists, who have often been explicit in rejecting custom and tradition, nevertheless have retained some historical sensibilities in expressing their moral and religious judgments. In this way the feelings about past restraints or concerns have persisted in them even though they reacted strongly against the way such restraints have been formulated and expressed, or exercised. Secularization, as it is now appearing in modern societies, presumes to be a more radical and decisive change of stance in society. In the main it stems from a breach in the feeling-tone of a people, which, in turn, impels a break with the past on many issues. It remains to be seen, however, how decisive and thoroughgoing it can be in altering the culture's psychical ground out of which sensibilities and valuations emerge. India's secularization, as we have observed, is at present ambiguous in this respect, since some expressions of it convey more of a liberal and modernist spirit in Indian culture than the radical departure from the historical ethos commonly associated with secularism; while other expressions of it take a more decisive form of rejection and relinquishment.

One must face the fact, I think, that a serious wrench in the quality and feeling of life is occurring in modern cultures wherever secular currents have been set in motion, countering historical or traditional ways of life. There is no blinking this fact. It is, of course, important that those who attend to the over-all structures of thought in a society see ways by which these new events or emphases may be assimilated to older ways of thinking, even as the latter are summoned to take cognizance of what is pertinent or imperative in the innovating and revolutionary occurrences within the culture's present history. In time such efforts may heal the breach as renascent and revolutionary developments partake of what is indigenous to the culture's history. They may also create the necessary bridges over which tradition-bound devotees of the society may pass into the promised land of the new age. But for some, this is not a present reality. And for them, secularism can mean only a wave of dissolution.

Whether it is a wave of dissolution, or of cultural renewal, one must say that secularization is clearly a wave of the future in India.

In the West, we have come to think of your late Prime Minister, Mr. Nehru, as having been the spearhead of secularization in modern India. He, more than any other single person, seemed to express with eloquence and firmness the yearning in modern India to avail itself of the best that modern science and technology could offer, as fast as the Indian people could assimilate it and use it, in the hope of moving India toward an adequate state of well-being for all its people. He voiced this again and again—in his many public speeches, in his writings, notably in *Discovery of India,* and in casual interviews from time to time.

Unlike both Mahatma Gandhi and Dr. Radhakrishnan, Pandit Nehru took a skeptical view toward religions. His own bent of mind seemed to be so basically scientific and humanistic in spirit, that he was offended by what he regarded as naïve and visionary claims of both mythological and mystical expressions of religion. And he deplored the excesses of religious emotion and zeal.

There is a moving and enduring memento of his secular sensibilities in the Nehru house in New Delhi, in the form of a large, framed page taken from a longer document, which was written early in the 1950's. Among other things, this document contains detailed instructions for his burial without benefit of any religious ceremony. The forthrightness and candor of this statement I found very moving.

Yet a decade later a book appeared, entitled *The Mind of Mr. Nehru, 1960.* Excerpts from this book, reporting an interview between the Prime Minister and the author, R. K. Karanjia, were later quoted in an article by M. M. Thomas entitled "Nehru's Secularism—An Interpretation." In this interview, discussing the relevance of science and technology to India's problems, Mr. Nehru complains that "what appears to be wanting in these matters of science and technology is an ethical aspect, some spiritual solution."

When his interviewer taunted him, asking, "Is this not unlike the Nehru of yesterday, to talk in terms of ethical and spiritual solutions?" Mr. Nehru replied,

If you put it that way, my answer is Yes. I have changed. The emphasis on ethical and spiritual solutions is not unconscious. It is deliberate, quite deliberate. There are good reasons for it. First of all, apart from material development that is imperative, I believe that the human mind is hungry for something deeper in terms of moral and spiritual development without which all the material advance may not be worthwhile. . . .

The problem is that once a person's physical wants are satisfied— that is, he's got enough money, employment, a home and other essentials—then he ceases to have a sure function of life.

"He gets engulfed in a spiritual vacuum?" his questioner interrupted.

Yes, a spiritual vacuum. An emptiness of the spirit, the result of which is what you call the angry young men and women of our generation. . . .

There must be a new approach, a modern approach, a moral and ethical approach. I really do not know how to put it, but something of that nature. Otherwise there is no solution to this riddle. The whole thing degenerates into power-rivalries which beset the development of our scientific and technological age. And this, in my opinion, brings us to the crux of the whole matter.[5]

Mr. Nehru never veered from his lifelong conviction that religions, in their preoccupation with mysteries and mythologies, neglected the immediate social tasks at hand, and often were obstructive of the social vision needed to deal with the problems of the day. In this sense he remained aloof from organized faiths as such; yet it becomes clear that, in his deeper sensibilities, he shared the response of serious minds to the spiritual dimension of existence, however defined, however much he may have pressed for a secular policy in the public life of India. Perhaps Shri Thomas's characterization of his view as "an Open Secularism" is a happy one, for it expresses the sensibilities at work in his view, even as it points up the clarity and decisiveness of its direction.

One may say, I think, that the Indian experience at this period of its history has been uniquely fortunate in having resources of the spirit in the person of its public figures. These men—you know their names—brought to the secularizing processes at work in modern society, at a time when crucial national decisions were being made, the kind of

[5] M. M. Thomas, "Nehru's Secularism—An Interpretation," *Religion and Society*, IX, 1 (March 1962), 10-11.

sanity and human amplitude of spirit which could mediate, and thus preserve, the moral fiber of the culture's spiritual heritage. Secularism in your country, therefore, particularly in its public exercise, as your President has observed, tends not to have the negative tone or implication which attend it in other cultures. Rather it has the connotation of cultural reclamation, a spirit of applying that spiritual heritage to necessary work at hand. This is most fortunate in some respects. In other respects, say in relating the issue of secularization in this country to its occurrences in other cultures, it may be less fortunate; for it may mislead the Indian mind into becoming unduly sanguine in its assumptions and expectations with regard to other secularized societies. For secularization is not everywhere motivated by cultural reclamation, nor is it a mediating influence, giving living force to an inherited faith. And with these more ominous secular currents being encountered both within and without the bounds of India's national life, it becomes a question whether India's present fortunate connotation of the secular mind can endure, or whether it will persist only as long as present transitions in its culture remain in process.

Some of the more angular and menacing aspects of this problem, particularly as they are beginning to appear in the West, will come before us as we consider various forms of secularization later.

Tentatively, then, we may summarize our observations thus far by saying that secularism in India arose simultaneously with the drive toward Indian nationalism and cultural renewal. It provided a political formula for conceiving of the cultural realities within a national framework. It is difficult, therefore, to think of secularism in India apart from nationalistic aspirations and the program of reform consonant with it.

II

Secularism in the West on the other hand was more diverse in origin, and thus today is more ambiguous in meaning and implication. It is true that secularization under some aspects had political origins in the struggle for freedom among Nonconformists in England, and specifically in the rise of the American Constitution. In this context it was explicitly a political issue, giving rise to the doctrine of the separation of church and state. For the wider, cultural aspect of secularism in the West one must look to the rise of the scientific movement and to developments in thought accompanying it. Here a real disruption in the mythos of the West was to occur; thus secularism in the West took on emotional overtones that were to give it a characteristic turn, peculiar to its cultural history. In this context, secularism was not, as in India, an expedient or instrumental means of realizing a nationalist outlook, but a more substantive upheaval in the structure of modern consciousness itself and in the human psyche, and thus was charged with traumatic energies of revolt and rejection. In turning to the West, then, we come upon a more complicated picture of secularization. And in recent years, with the rapid advance in technology, automation, and nuclear pursuits, the term secular has become even more clouded in meaning, and its usage more ambiguous. This was not so earlier in our history. At that time the term "secular" had a singular meaning. It meant "nonreligious"— that which opposed the "sacred." And to Western minds in most cases, this meant "non-Christian." The onus in these instances was on the secularist. He had strayed from the prevailing community of believers, and had rejected their consensus of belief. On his own initiative, or through a moral relapse, he had become an outsider, a secularist.

Beginning with the seventeenth century in Europe, certain intellectual and cultural processes were set in motion which were to widen the scope of secularizing forces in the West. Arnold Toynbee cites the years beginning with the latter half of the seventeenth century as a time when Western culture as a whole first turned toward secularization.

This leaven of secularization which began at the close of the seventeenth century and spread progressively from one stratum of Western society to another till it had permeated the whole mass, culminated in the discrediting of the West's Christian heritage and the elevation of a technical civilization that has only tenuous connections at best with the Christian heritage and ethos.[6]

What Toynbee has in mind here specifically is the changing outlook that took form under Newton and Descartes, and which in time solidified into a thoroughgoing scientific naturalism. Secularism in this context was not so much a matter of individuals breaking away from existing religious and cultural beliefs and practices as that of a new community of mind emerging, centering around new disciplines and forms of inquiry that were to challenge, and eventually to supersede, this prevailing Christian consensus in major centers of learning and scholarship. With the rise of industrialization in England that was to follow, and its extension to other parts of Europe and America, what had begun as a mode of inquiry in pure science merged with the technical demands of industry until science, together with industry, laid the ground for a new technological civilization in the West. What finally emerged in Europe and in the United States of America during the nineteenth century was a full-blown modernistic consciousness that had all but cut its ties with the historical legacy of past centuries. Science and

[6] Arnold Toynbee, *An Historian's Approach to Religion*, New York: Oxford University Press, 1956.

industry were the formidable molders of this new consciousness; and in the mode of life they created, a new ethos
within Western culture itself was to emerge. Thus at the
close of the nineteenth century, secularism in Europe and in
the United States was rather steadily recognizable and definable. Secularism was taken to mean this explicit form of
scientific naturalism that expressed full allegiance to the
truth of the sciences and the demands of industry, and commitment to those procedures in education and other institutions of society which could implement these scientific findings and serve these technical demands.

But before we identify western secularism wholly, or too
readily, with nineteenth-century scientific naturalism, or
with any other modernistic creed, we should note its larger,
more pervasive spirit, manifest among many diverse groups,
but always as a drive toward enlightenment amidst restrictive and zealous forces of society.

In its finest expression, secularism in the West has meant
a sense of impatience and restraint among disciplined and
sensitive minds of the culture, resisting the uncontrolled
passion and zeal of religious cults and individuals. In the
spirit of the Renaissance man or of the eighteenth-century
liberal, this kind of secularist has been dedicated to the freedom and refinement of the human spirit, and thus has been
resistant to any corporate religious or political influence that
threatened to suppress or to degrade the stature of man.
This kind of secular spirit has been of immeasurable value in
our Western history. It has contributed mightily and mag-
nificently to the art and literature of Western experience.
It has been a persistent, critical, and acidulous strand within
Western philosophy, countering ontological excesses when
they minimized the dignity of man in deference to abstract
authorities, and demanding a serious reckoning with the
powers of creativity and responsible action inherent in this

human dimension. This form of the secular spirit, more than any other, perhaps, has been aware of and attentive to the ambiguities of man's higher dedications, and to the gross evil lurking within or behind religious zeal. William Ernest Hocking, the American philosopher, once characterized religion as a huge potency of ambiguous meaning and value. Western history, as indeed, your own national history in India, has known the depths and magnitude of the evil that can issue from religious zeal and dedication under certain circumstances. It *is* a huge potency; and its purposes as well as its explicit acts can be fraught with ambiguous passions that are deceptive and destructive. Wherever the secular spirit has raised its voice to temper and to discipline these reckless outbursts of passion within a culture, it has itself been a spiritual force in man of a most significant order.

It is at this point that one begins to appreciate the distinction that is currently being made between *religions* and the life of the spirit. Religions, presumably, are the exemplars of this life of the spirit, and the means of its nurture. However, they can also become the betrayers of its deepest and highest notions, and thus be made a corrupting influence, not only within the culture of man, but within the larger domain of the Spirit that would relate man to a good not his own. For this reason the secular spirit, both within and without the religious community, can be a salutary influence upon religion itself, demanding that it be true to its inherent character and mission.

Religions have a way, too, of betraying what is inherently significant and creative in man, himself—the life of the mind, the capacity for artistic expression and the love of beauty. In the West, both an anti-intellectual drive and a suspicion of the artistic sense in man have played havoc with the Christian faith in certain periods and places, turning religion in these instances against education, causing it to reject and to combat the sciences as a deadly foe, and to repudiate every concern with the arts as a threat to its moral existence. I shall want to examine this form of religious pathology later. It is enough at this point to note this tendency in order to understand the secular spirit that is evoked by it as a counter effect within the culture.

There is, to be sure, some basis for concern about the impoverishing, even debasing, effects of higher learning and the pursuit of the arts upon the spirit of man. Education and art, dissociated from what have generally been regarded as ultimate claims upon man's destiny, can become narrowing enterprises, expressive of man in his most limited capacity as a manipulator of mechanisms, or as an irresponsible and indolent individual, indulging his fancies. But they need not be, and they generally do not become so. Nevertheless, there is enough of this delimiting or debasing influence issuing from intellectual and artistic communities to convince the religious zealot that he is justified in fighting against all expressions of it.

The secularism that arises in a culture out of protest against the excesses and extravagances of religious zeal and passion, however, can itself become afflicted with this form of invalidism. The wounds of its resentments and anguish fester and yield up an embittered reaction against all things religious. Secularism itself may thus become a form of uncontrolled zeal that carries its own poisonous venon into the life of the community. Thus, what initially arose as a sane, disciplined resistance to the folly of religious zeal dissolves into a counter-movement of zealots, bent on destroying all religion, but in the process, becoming itself a religion of demonic proportions. Secularism then assumes the specific character and intent of an anti-religion drive, and in this form it presents an ominous prospect, not only for religions, but for the cultural life of man. Western history, particularly from the late nineteenth century on, has suffered from this kind of doctrinaire repudiation of religion. For in its disavowals, not only have the pathologies of religious zeal been opposed, but the sensibilities implicit in our idealistic and humanistic legacy have likewise been rejected, thereby debasing the image of man to such an extent that he could readily be made the pawn of a power struggle, and thereby made expendable without protest or conscience. When this debasement of the human spirit has assumed the proportions of a crusade, as in certain stages of Communist history, or of mass hysteria, as in the Nazi uprising, the most heinous crimes against segments of humanity have been perpetrated.

The drive against religion is thus never just an attack upon explicit religious institutions and practices, but a disavowal of sensibilities and expectations with regard to individual man which, in theory at least, have enhanced the image of man and his social status. This correlation of the culture's religious history with the ultimate dignity of man is by no means unambiguous. Instances to the contrary can readily be cited, such as the attempts to give biblical justification of human slavery among certain Southern churchmen; or the overt enslavement of human beings as factory workers among pious Northern industrialists prior to the rise of trade unions in the United States. But these discrepancies, along with their own distinctive disclosures of depravity, stand repudiated by the more sensitive and prophetic legacy of this religious history, which, one may say, has been the more enduring, if not always the more pervasive, form of its witness.

The ferment of antireligion as a crusading spirit, though it exists today, is less in evidence than it was two or three decades ago. In the 1930's and early 1940's, or even as early as the late 1920's, a vigorous, self-conscious drive was in progress in several cultures of the world, bent upon uprooting religion. I recall writing an article at that time on "Why Modern Cultures Are Uprooting Religion."[7] Other theologians, impressed by the intensity of this antireligion ferment, speculated about the prospects of religious leaders and their devotees the world around having to withdraw into modern catacombs in order to survive; the sense of threat was that acute. Cultures like modern Turkey had already eradicated historical religious traditions on a radical scale, seeking to transform its society *in toto* by compelling it to assume a modern dress.[8] Other modern cultures, notably Soviet Russia, were waging open warfare against established religion, seeking to dislodge its hold upon society in the hope of replacing its influence with that of secular institutions and customs. In this Russia has been only partially successful.[9] Even in a culture like China, prior to its communist era, antireligion tendencies were vigorously at work in the 1920's and 1930's; and these were being encouraged, even promoted, by high-minded intellectuals who saw in religious traditions a formidable deterrent to applying the modernist spirit to educational, literary, and social activities. One of the prominent leaders in this drive to uproot religion in the interest of modernizing Chinese culture was the eminent Chinese philosopher, Dr. Hu Shih, later to become China's ambassador to the United States. In Hu Shih's behalf it should be said that his motives in countering the hold of religious traditions upon Chinese culture were of a high intellectual order. They were consonant with a general

[7] *Christendom*, VI (1941), 194-204.
[8] See Henry Allen, *The Turkish Transformation*, Chicago: University of Chicago Press, 1935.
[9] See N. Berdyaev, *Origin of Russian Communism* (paperback edition), Ann Arbor: University of Michigan Press, 1960; C. Grunwald, *The Churches and the Soviet Union*, New York: Macmillan, 1962; M. Spinka, *The Church and the Russian Revolution*, New York: Macmillan, 1927; and M. Spinka, *Christianity Confronts Communism*, New York: Harper, 1937.

movement of mind in the West which had long been impatient with the suppressive influence of religious traditions and their consequent resistance to social change. Dr. Hu Shih was the moving spirit behind what was then called the Chinese Renaissance.[10] He had translated some of the Chinese classics into the language of the people, and had committed himself to writing his own works in this common tongue. He had publicly released his son from any deference or homage to himself which tradition had laid upon him. His every concern was to release his countrymen from the bondage of the past and from institutions and practices that nurtured such allegiance to the mores of the past. I well recall a memorable occasion at the University of Chicago in 1933 at which Dr. Hu Shih dramatically declared his views to an American audience. Historians of religion from various colleges and universities had gathered to interpret the role of religion in modern cultures and to assess the possibilities of the various religions assuming such a role in the new life of the world that was then emerging. Several eminent scholars from East and West had spoken, giving their views on this theme. Dr. Hu Shih was the principal speaker at its closing session. Addressing himself to the theme of the conference, Dr. Hu Shih opened his remarks with the statement, "The most important contribution that the religions of the world could make to modern societies in the world today would be to commit suicide." Though these words were said with the calm and detachment of a philosopher and scholar, nevertheless they registered with nuclear effect. They were shocking, not because they were unexpected, or wholly alien to the thinking of many present, but because they expressed so openly and candidly what

[10] See Hu Shih, *The Chinese Renaissance*, Chicago: The University of Chicago Press, 1934.

many knew to be a widely shared sentiment that was then gathering power as a social force.

It may well be that many of our contemporaries would readily echo Dr. Hu Shih's words, "Let the religions of the world commit suicide!" But that sentiment appears to be less of a social force in our time than it was a generation ago. Certainly the vigorous effort among established leaders to uproot religions, which was so assertive in the 1930's and 1940's, or even earlier, has in the main subsided. Something in the nature of events following the last World War has impelled political forces to assume a more negotiable policy in dealing with religious communities. It may be true, too, that many government officials, or even heads of governments today, would like to emulate the transformation of Turkey, relinquishing with one firm edict the hold of religious traditions over its people. In the main, however, the process appears to be in an opposite direction, either re-examining the resources of these religious traditions with a view to becoming selectively and intelligently critical in response to their mores as modern men; or forthrightly establishing a secular state, not necessarily with a view to suppressing or tyrannizing over religions, but conversely, out of a concern to arbitrate between them, and thus to assure the peace among its people, as they strive to live together with their differences. There are, of course, relapses into religious establishments, as in Burma, where Buddhism has recently assumed ascendancy over other religious faiths in the nation, and in Pakistan, where Islam has been made the directing force in government and culture; but these are hardly representative procedures of modern nations. Reinstating religion as a directing source of political judgment and action carries considerable risk in the present passion-ridden world situation; but if the danger does not get out of hand, such an arrangement could be an interesting experiment in the conscious pursuit of a religious culture within the ethos of modern times.[11]

Among the major democracies there appears to be no sound or salutary alternative to the secular state, understood as a negotiator in the interest of peace and justice between religious groups within a single nation. The secular state, as India and the United States know it, is first and foremost a creation of the people through their elected representatives. It is consciously devised by citizens, sharing themselves in a religious commitment, to neutralize or to evade possible, and perhaps inescapable, tensions of partisanship between the cults in the exercise of the affairs of state. It is further devised to insure a just relation between the state and all religions, and to such a degree that is manageable by the authority and prestige of the state, to assure a liveable peace between them. To these ends, the secular state seeks to dissociate the decisions and policies of state from religious considerations, influences, or representations and to guard against interfering with the exercise of religious faiths by individuals or groups of believers. Secularization in this sense is not directed against the personal embodiment of a faith, or

---

[11] The danger implicit in modern forms of religious cultures has been highlighted by the recent conflict between Pakistan and India. Pakistan has urged that a plebiscite be held in Kashmir to determine whether its people are to be ruled by Pakistan or India. Their readiness to have such a plebiscite held no doubt stems from the fact that the people living in Kashmir are predominantly Moslem, and it would seem reasonable to assume that, given a plebiscite, the majority would choose to be ruled by Pakistan, a Moslem state. India, on the other hand, fears this solution, not simply on the grounds that it would lose Kashmir, but that in losing it on grounds of religious affiliation, India itself conceivably would erupt with religious revolts, re-enacting the very events of 1946 and 1947 that initially gave rise to the split between Pakistan and India. A religious culture such as Pakistan may not necessarily intrude the religious issue insofar as its internal national life is concerned, but when tensions or conflict between itself and another nation arises, the fact of its being a Moslem state cannot fail to evoke religious feelings under some circumstances.

its exercise by individuals active in government, or even by the national leader himself. Thus the mores of the faith, or the ethos of its tradition and history, are not necessarily excluded from the exercise of government. Although these mores may not rise to the surface as overt arguments or principles in the deliberations of a political assembly, they are very apt to be present and pervasive in the presuppositions, sentiments, and objectives that motivate and direct such deliberations. In short, the mythos of religions in any culture reaches to the depths of the human psyche and are not readily extricated from the scene of thought and action by deliberate legislative acts or agreement. It is important to recognize this fact in assessing the cultural effects of the secular state. I shall have more to say on these points when I deal directly with the concept of the secular state.

III

Anyone who surveys the total cultural scene within modern societies today soon comes to discover that the process of secularization in our time extends beyond these conscious and forthright acts to suppress or to displace religion. For secularization in modern form is no longer just a rival frame of reference or outlook, challenging or defying historical religious faiths. It is, rather, a condition of life that steadily invades the processes of society and family life, feeding upon the apathy and indifference of people to historic sensibilities and religious principles. This is a more deadly form of secularism, principally because it is so pervasive and presumably hidden, and because it assumes no clear sense of focus at any one point. Conceivably this form of secularization is a by-product of a mode of existence that has been created by a well-meaning and much-needed concentration upon the concern with physical well-being. This is an ironical twist of events. The very efforts, through social analysis and social engineering, to improve man's lot and to relieve him of oppressive burdens that defeat his spirit, have, in many instances, notably in the West, relieved him also of the incentive to become a full human being, or to live for ends beyond his creature-comforts and the facilities that will assure them. In the words of your late Prime Minister Nehru, "once a person's physical wants are satisfied . . . he ceases to have a sure function of life."

We in the West have generally resented your taunts about our Western materialism, especially when you have done so by way of contrasting it with your own spirituality. For we are aware that this stricture upon our mode of life does not apply to the whole of our history, nor to every aspect of our present existence. And furthermore, we are not wholly convinced that these materially directed motives do not abound in the cultures of the East as well. Nevertheless, there is a disturbing truth implicit in this characterization of every culture that has awakened to the possibilities of improving the material life of man. And it is this disturbing truth that now looms, as I have said, upon the horizon of every present-day culture that has been caught up in this world-wide concern for well-being. Our experience in the West of seeing masses of human beings eschewing all concern with the sensitive and reflective ends of life in their preoccupation with things and machines, and the wonder they can perform, gives us pause as we contemplate this pattern of existence being emulated in one culture after another around the globe. The American philosopher, Ralph Waldo Emerson, looking out upon the rising industrialized scene in American communities a century or so ago, lamented, "Things are in the saddle, and ride mankind!" This lament haunts us still, and even more so as we visualize its increasing magnitude through technology, nuclear power, and automation; and as we sense its need in the wake of world-wide human poverty, hunger, and physical deprivation.

The secularization that issues from this preoccupation with machines in the interest of well-being is twofold: There is the loss of the human outreach as the concern with creature-comforts and the ease of living takes hold of men and women, along with the blurring of the image of man as machines and their massive power assume ascendancy in modern societies, rendering man himself ever more dependent upon their operation, and the resources they provide. This leads to a further form of secularization in modern cultures, a form of secularization to which I am particularly concerned to draw your attention: It is the secularization that follows, quite unwittingly in most instances, from the statistical method of the sciences and its application in modern industry and in other areas of society. Secularization in this sense is not an act of revolt or reaction, but a condition that befalls a people. Science and industry, working together, provide the tools, machines, and resources for carrying on the activities of a technological society, but they also provide consumer products on a mass scale which must be marketed; and this requires a mass market, which in turn gives rise to what has been tentatively termed "a mass culture."[12] Wherever a "mass culture" arises in response to the mass appeal of industries, the note of selectivity and sensibility in judgment tends to go out of a culture.[13] For in the

[12] See Normal Jacobs (ed.), *Culture for the Millions,* Boston: Beacon Press, 1964.
[13] This point became vivid to me in a conversation I had some years ago with a young lady from Mexico, who was in the United States pleading for some restraint upon American importers who had made a big business of marketing certain of the Mexican crafts in the United States. Something I had written in my *Seeds of Redemption* (1947) had led her to believe that I might be of help in encouraging such an effort. She reported that the publicized demand for certain articles had given rise to the mass production of them to the exclusion of everything else that their crafts-

industrialized society, beholden to a mass culture, such discrimination in taste and judgment is a luxury, except as it can be turned into a gimmick of mass appeal, and then the qualitative aspect of the article or articles thus exploited tends to be leveled out to conform to a prevailing mediocrity. No more serious threat to the spiritual life of democratic cultures exists today, in my judgment, than this contrived and highly organized procedure in modern industry to elevate mediocrity and to turn it to marketable ends. Its insidious influence has spread to all areas of society. The American poet, Randall Jarrell, in a scintillating essay called "A Sad Heart at the Supermarket," comments on the lines from Emerson that I quoted earlier, saying:

Things are in the saddle and ride mankind. Emerson could say more now: He could say they are in the theater and studio, and entertain mankind; are in the pulpit and preach to mankind. The values of business, in an overwhelmingly successful business society like our own, are reflected in every sphere: values which agree with them are reinforced, values which disagree are cancelled out or have lip-service paid to them. In business what sells is good, and that's the end of it—that is what *good* means.[14]

This judgment points up one of the most ominous aspects of the affluent societies of the West.

---

men might create. Craftsmen were being herded into factory-like centers to produce these particular articles. "Our craftsmen are becoming less and less artists or creative workmen, expressing the imaginative spirit of the Mexican people," she lamented. "They are being turned into factory workers, responsive only to the demands of exporters who must satisfy a mass market. We are doing what we can in Mexico," she continued, "to urge our craftsmen to remain artists with some concern to transcend this mass exploitation of our crafts; but we need the help of people in this country who can educate both importers and consumers to give our craftsmen the freedom to be creative, rather than mere puppets in a mass industry." On examination, one would find, no doubt, that Indian crafts, as others the world over, are being subjected to this kind of secularization.

[14] Jacobs, op. cit. p. 101.

The reverse of this situation can also dissipate the spiritual dimension of human living, deteriorating into purposelessness and loss of function in life. Instead of apathy and indifference which so often follows from affluence and well-being, there is disillusionment and despair, following from experiences of dislocation and deprivation. Many instances of this have occurred out of the disruptions of war, forced migrations of people under attack, revolutions, and other radical forms of cultural change. Notable instances of this have been occurring in the new nations, as in modern Africa. What we see happening in some of these new nations is, in one sense, very old. It is as old as the transition from the bedouin life of the desert to settled agricultural living, or from farm life to the life of the cities. Yet the form it assumes in some of the new states of Africa carries a poignancy and sense of desolateness that is peculiar to the revolutionary circumstances in which it is now occurring. A glimpse of this new kind of secularization appeared in a revealing article on "The Fabric of African Cultures," by Ezekiel Mphahlele, in a recent issue of *Foreign Affairs*. Here are some excerpts from that article:

The music floats in the night across the vast complex of African townships (or "locations" as they are called in South Africa). It is heard in all parts of this black metropolis because it is a loud and robust music. The singing dancers—all young men and women and boys and girls—stamp it out on the street each night for a whole month before a wedding until it sounds as if the musicians were trapped in a sunset-to-midnight orgy. . . .

. . . .

Here the city boy and girl have come in at a certain point of cultural continuity, a continuity that is being lived by country folk. The music is still intact; only the lyrics are drawn from city life. . . .

And so an urban culture has evolved. It is an escape route for a people on the run; but it is the only virile culture in South Africa, beside which the derivative and fragmented one of the whites (English and Afrikaans) looks sterile; it is something that sustains the black man. . . .

. . . .

Among the 4,000,000 Africans who are now urbanized, there are several who maintain links with their people in the country, because they are relative newcomers in the towns. There is also a large population of female domestics who live on employers' premises and are in constant touch with their country folk. They are highly sophisticated, dress smartly in pay-while-you-wear clothes, but are not involved in the rough-and-tumble existence of location people. They carry back to their "reserves" transistor radios and gramophones, concertinas, mouth organs, town gadgets and foods, and new-style clothing. Those who envy them go to the towns to look for work, or allow themselves to be recruited for mine labor. The system of migrant labor is thus consolidated. The intercourse between town and country is thus established and maintained. Family life is broken in the process. But the human traffic keeps moving, like droves of ants, with a tragic inevitability. The lives of the 3,000,000 Africans in the rural areas have consequently been disturbed. The land does not hold much for them any more. The members of the family who have gone to the towns will send money when they can and when they have not been swallowed up by urban life. . . .

Then there are the 3,000,000 Africans working on white people's farms as labor tenants. They have, like the town folk, cut their tribal moorings, and owe no allegiance to a chief. Here cultural life seems to turn around in circles, finding no nourishment from either rural or urban life. Something about these people hangs in suspension, as if waiting for a fulfillment, the energy for which they are incapable of generating.[15]

Secularization here is compounded by the mixture of the ingredients, by the contradiction of moods, registering revolt and nostalgia, a mood of alienation mingling with a sense of belonging under new circumstances, of disorienta-

[15] Ezekiel, Mphahlele, "The Fabric of African Cultures," *Foreign Affairs*, XLII, 4 (July 1964), 614-16.

tion at having been uprooted from familiar, yet coercive surroundings, coupled with a new-found freedom that is heady and exhilarating, though as yet unproved, and, in a way, unassured. But it is no simple transition from village to city. The gap in some instances is from recent recollections of a tribal mode of life, with its faiths and phantasies, to the sophistications of a completely technological way of living, in which all traditions and religious legacies are expendable in the swift pace of getting on. Of what concern is primitivity to the modern man? asks the cultural anthropologist, or the historian of religions, concerned to bridge the gap between the studies of antiquity and the current cultural revolutions. For them it may be an academic question that invites speculative inquiry. For these African young people it is the poignant and ineradicable fact of family connections, and the haunting desire to belong to one world without relinquishing another.

Peter B. Hammond has described a similar transition leading to a modified secularization of life among Africans who have been removed from their native habitat. These are the Mossi villagers who are at work on the Niger Irrigation Project in the French Sudan. Says Hammond, speaking of these changes,

Arriving at the Niger project, they fail to find the institutions upon which they have always depended for their security; they find instead a natural environment governed by forces they do not know. Their water supply is no longer dependent on the supernatural controls of the earth custodians but comes from a dam built by Europeans. They are socially isolated from their kinsmen and their ancestral spirits in the Yatenga, and they derive little comfort from the presence of fellow Mossi with whom they have neither consanguineal nor affinal relationship.[16]

[16] William R. Bascom and Melville J. Herskovits (eds.), *Continuity and Change in African Cultures*, Chicago: University of Chicago Press, 1959, p. 252.

But here an interesting transfer of religious allegiance occurs:

Rather than diminishing their belief in their own religion, it only
convinces the Mossi colonists that the forces of the natural order
are different in their new habitat and accordingly must be controlled in a different way. Finding the indigenous inhabitants of
the French Sudan, the Bambara, to be zealous Moslems, the Mossi
settlers have accepted Islam as the religion of their new country.
Confident that their religious obligations in the Yatenga will be
taken care of by the elders who have remained behind, and with
some pressure from those who have already become Moslemized,
new arrivals rapidly embrace Islam as the system by which the
supernatural forces governing their new environment can be
manipulated.[17]

Yet this proves to be but a partial solution to their problems. As Hammond observes, "their acceptance of Islam"
under these conditions "has been as superficial as it has been
rapid." And when they return to their former kinsmen new
problems arise. These are reinforced and accentuated by the
"pattern of residential grouping" that is made necessary by
the new situation at the project, which, "in the absence of
the lineage" is meaningless to the Mossi colonists. Their shift
in religious adherence does not really help them with this
problem, for it does not meet the African's difficulties
caused by the changed social organization. At this point the
isolation from their kinsmen and the protection of their ancestral spirits experienced in the traditional kinship organization produces grave social as well as psychical disturbances. And it is in this situation of people being isolated and
rejected that the ferment of secularization sets in, not by
anyone's choice, but as a way of adapting to a situation imposed by new circumstances.

The problem of secularization in modern cultures is a

[17] Ibid. p. 253.

complex, social process, assuming various expressions and dimensions. The source tends to give character and direction to the secularizing process at work. Where the source is a disruption in the controlling ethos of a culture, motivated by a conscious reaction against inherited religious beliefs, as in the early phase of the modern period in the West, secularization is identified as being simply a relapse from religious loyalties and convictions. Under other circumstances, where it arises more positively out of a new social vision of the culture, it is identified as a liberating and cleansing force within society, preparing it for a serious encounter with demands of the new age. It can arise, too, simply out of the critical demand for religious toleration in situations where competing religious forces frustrate or threaten the social well-being of a people. The secular state, as we have noted, has been the outcome of this demand in certain instances, serving as a negotiating and regulating agency within society, in behalf of its larger citizenry.

But secularization is also appearing unwittingly in modern cultures, being not so much a purposive or consciously directed movement, as a condition of life that befalls a people, a kind of pathology following from certain preoccupations associated with scientific and technological pursuits, and with procedures accompanying industrialization; or with widespread circumstances of dislocation, wherein the once familiar and inherited directives of life become vague and ineffectual.

Secularization is thus as many-sided as the sources that produce it, and the assessment of it, like one's interpretation, requires that one be alert to the ambiguity of its meaning and intent within any culture. There is, however, one clear issue that secularization poses wherever it appears, under whatever conditions it may appear; that is the role and status of religious sensibilities in any culture. Secularization presents either a challenge or a threat to these sensibilities. It shall be my concern in the lectures that follow to explore these various aspects of secularization in modern cultures and to come to some judgments concerning this basic issue. The first four will treat specific forms of secularization; the last two will inquire into the significance of religious sensibilities and wonder in the face of modern secularization, and in an age in which science and technology along with industrialization are clearly in the ascendancy.

Secularization of the Modern State

Today we are to consider secularization as it appears in the policies of the modern secular state. Some of you, no doubt, are familiar with Professor Nilakanta Sastri's interesting essay, giving an historical analysis of the Concept of a Secular State.[1] Professor Sastri suggests that the notion of a secular state is essentially modern, though he finds historical antecedents of its development both in India and in the West. Speaking of the West, he says, prior to "the declaration of American Independence and the French Revolution, when democracy and the sovereignty of the people became the accepted foundation of a modern political life," the pattern of monarchical states with some form of affirmation of divine right prevailed. He finds a similar correlation between religion and the state existing from antiquity in the East, with the laws of the state in India deriving from the ancient Vedas. Professor Sastri points out, however, that throughout India's history, notably in the period prior to A.D. 1200, but even after Moslem rule developed, as in the sixteenth

[1] K. A. Nilakanta Sastri, *The Concept of a Secular State*, Madras: S. Viswanathan, n.d.

century under Akbar, a marked note of religious toleration persisted. And this, he seems to suggest, has implications consonant with the modern notion of the secular state in that it provided a political and cultural atmosphere conducive to religious differences, and the freedom to affirm and to practice a religion other than the one dominantly favored. Obviously it would be a mistake to equate religious toleration, even historically, with secularism in government; however, I think Professor Sastri is justified in suggesting that with this legacy of religious toleration in Indian history, modern India has the historical precedent for giving to the notion of secularization a constructive meaning which can indirectly, yet effectively, serve the present situation.[2]

The concept of the secular state within any nation presents problems peculiar to the cultural situation, following from the evolution of its political institutions and from de-

---

[2] While in India, my attention was called to an article by Sadashiv Hari Godbole of Poona, in which he advances the thesis that the principle of the secular government goes as far back in Indian history as Asoka, the First Emperor of India, and, through him, to the ancient Vedas. In making this point he also stresses what President Radhakrishnan has asserted, namely, that secularism in India has a spiritual connotation. However, instead of presenting secularism as a reconception of India's spiritual tradition, Godbole is concerned to show its traditional precedent. He points out that the Wheel, which appears on the national flag of modern India as the emblem of secular democracy, is in fact an explicit assertion of the spiritual emphasis of Indian secularism. "The spokes of the wheel," he writes, "may be said to denote and symbolize synthesis of all religions." Furthermore, he suggests, the fact that this symbol expressed in the wheel was taken from the Asoka Pillar in Sarna identifies contemporary Indian secularism not only with the tolerant era of the First Emperor of India, but with "the high principles of polity taught in the Vedas, by which Emperor Asoka's policy of Government was dictated." Thus he concludes that "The ideal of our Government of establishing a secular state is quite in accordance with the conception of a sovereign state as directed by our ancient Bharatiya civilization." (This article by Godbole, entitled "Vedic Search-Light on The Carving of 'Asoka Wheel,'" first appeared in a Marathi paper, Lokrajya, published in Poona, August 22, 1947. It later appeared in English in The Poona Daily News, August 17, 1951.)

velopments in its religious traditions and customs. It is thus difficult, and possibly fruitless, to deal with the concept of the secular state as if it conveyed a singular and specific meaning, applicable to any modern situation. Abstractly speaking, one can say that a secular state is one that assumes a role of neutrality with regard to religion and to the affairs of religious communities, in contrast to a theocratic state; or to one involved in church establishment, which formally and openly incorporates religious dictates and directives in the exercise of government. But the moment one begins to think concretely about this distinction, one discovers how difficult it is to find terms, conditions, or policies that accurately or adequately express this role of neutrality within a specific culture. This difficulty has been admirably demonstrated by Donald E. Smith, the American professor of Political Science in the University of Rhode Island, in an impressive volume on *India As A Secular State*.[3] This book represents a thorough canvassing of all aspects of the problem of a secular government in action within the Indian situation. It reviews the history of the problem, touching upon antecedents from ancient times, but gives more careful attention to developments in the modern period, beginning with the formation of the Indian National Congress in 1885. It then focuses study upon the succession of events following India's independence in 1947, analyzing the articles of the Constitution bearing upon the principle of secularization. For any one wishing to become acquainted with events giving rise to this exciting and impressive period of India's national history, it is a source book of great value. The spirit of the book is eminently fair and constructive, and its author expresses a genuine concern not only to understand the difficult problems attending the cultural revo-

[3] Princeton: Princeton University Press, 1964.

lution in this country, but to be of help in dealing with these problems.

Yet the book illustrates a fallacy in approaching the problem of the secular state as well. Professor Smith begins his study in this volume by offering a definition of the secular state. A secular state, he writes, provides for three conditions: (1) freedom of religion, as it concerns the relationship between religion and the individual; (2) the opportunity for citizenship for individuals with rights and duties that are not affected by the individual's religious beliefs; and (3) the separation of state and religion, as this affects the organizational aspects of religious communities. In this form, he observes, it is commonly experienced as the separation of church and state.

One has only to ponder the implications of these three aspects to recognize how closely they accord with the emergence of the secular state in the West, particularly in the United States, and how awkwardly they apply to the situation in modern India. Professor Smith is fully aware of this discrepancy, and refers to it frequently throughout his discussion of India's problems. He points out, for example, that the role of individuals in religion is not as pronounced in religions of the East as it has been in Western faiths, particularly those in the United States of America. And he recognizes further that, precisely because both Hinduism and Islam have evolved as communal faiths, embracing the total sphere of living, the effort to define the role of citizenship, answerable to the state, independently of religious loyalties, presents difficult problems. But more serious difficulties arise in connection with his last criterion, the separation of state and religion. For one thing, the more manageable expression of such a cleavage as separation of church and state simply does not have the clear and ready connotation which every American would recognize; for the reason that the

concept of church, and the precise ecclesiastical organization and focus it implies, has no simple counterpart in Hinduism or Islam. It is true, as Professor Smith remarks, that
certain organized groups within the Hindu community do
resemble the pattern of the church as it is known in the
West; for example, Hindu monastic institutions commonly
referred to as *maths*, or the Ramakrishna Mission.[4] But these
exceptional parallels do not help much in dealing with the
Indian situation as a whole. Furthermore, in the absence of
a specific focus, the separation of state and Hinduism, for
example, cannot be readily effected without incurring other
complications. One illustration which is cited is the need for
governmental participation in religious festivals involving
extensive pilgrimages. Without such governmental participation, it is argued, religious festivals would become a threat
to public health. If one were to take these last two criteria at
face value, and to make them determinative, then one would
have to conclude that the concept of the secular state is but
an ideal in India, if, in fact, it is ever possible of realization.

But Professor Smith's way of establishing the concept of
the secular state is made to appear even more doctrinaire
when he generalizes upon its application to other cultural
experiments in secularizing the state. For example, he observes, by way of illustrating the application of his criteria,
that, while Soviet Russia has achieved a church-state separation, "Soviet Russia is not a secular state."[5] He reaches
this conclusion because it does not satisfy the first criterion,
namely, freedom of religion. This comes as something of a
shock to one who has thought of secularization in more
common-sense terms. For if Soviet Russia is not a secular
state, what modern nation is? But you see what Professor
Smith was about in his analysis. He was attempting to pre-

4 Ibid. p. 112ff.
5 Ibid. p. 20.

sent a constructive program of secularization in government, and toward this end, he defined what he considered to be the *ideal* secular state, an ideal which he himself observes "is perfectly achieved in no country."[6] And then this interesting statement follows:

> The United States comes close [i.e. to achieving this ideal] but there are still obvious anomalies as well as important issues yet to be decided. Any modern state within the liberal democratic traditions will have many of the characteristics of a secular state. The United Kingdom, for example, can be regarded as a secular state in many respects, although the existence of a state church goes contrary to one important part of our definition.[7]

Now what I mean to question here is the abstract approach to formulating the concept of the secular state, recognizing that the moment such a formulation is accomplished it remains a remote ideal, suspended in mid-air, rather than a tool of inquiry for understanding the realities of cultural change.

Secularization, even as a process within modern nations, is pluralistic. That is, it is taking place under a variety of conditions and against backgrounds of religious and cultural traditions that run the gamut from the primitive to the highly developed forms of civilization. In some instances, as in certain regions of Africa, one sees the mores of tribal religions in juxtaposition with constitutional deliberations, aiming to bring a community into a participating relationship with a world community that confronts the promise and peril of a technological and nuclear age. In other cultures, and this I would think might describe the circumstances of India and Soviet Russia, as well as the United States, venerable traditions of religious history along with a

[6] Ibid. p. 8.
[7] Ibid.

highly cultivated and sophisticated lore in literature, philosophy, and the arts confront this new age of power and inventiveness.

The folly of rigidly applying a theoretical definition of the secular state to an actual experiment in secularization is again demonstrated in a brilliantly executed analysis of the Indian Constitution, *The Concept of the Secular State*, by Ved Prakesh Luthera.[8] Luthera also finds it convenient to take Western secularism as being definitive of the term, and to regard the American Constitution, with its separation of church and state, as normative and ideal. He then has only to show that the Indian Constitution lacks the specific clauses and provisions that this ideal secularism of the United States employs to come to the conclusion that India is not a secular state. There is value in the kind of analysis which Luthera has set forth. It brings out, for one thing, the complexity of the problem with which the Indian framers of their Constitution were dealing. It also reveals their wisdom in dealing with it. Had they proceeded in the doctrinaire manner which Luthera seems to favor, India would have emerged with a Constitution that, in theory, stood in defiance of all religious faiths. Had the Indian government been saddled with such a Constitution, it would have been obliged to abandon its role as mediator or negotiator between the faiths, and would instead have loomed as their common adversary. And in accomplishing its ends in such a role it might well have yielded to practices approximating religious persecution. In any case, it acts as a secular government might have been so interpreted. With India's religious history, only a marginal beginning toward a clarification of the functions of the state in relation to religious issues was possible. The one clear position these Indian statesmen could

[8] Calcutta: Oxford University Press, 1964.

take was that they would not elevate one religion above all others in the substantive sense that Pakistan had done, or as Burma was to do in making Buddhist interests and policies sovereign in shaping the laws of the land. Practically, Indian secularization was to become compromised by India's historical involvement in the communal life of Hinduism; but the secular state of India was to steer a course that sought to minimize this involvement, rather than to accentuate it as a principle and policy of state. In short, it would not become a theocratic state. Decisions of state were to be determined on the basis of the needs and well-being of its entire citizenry, insofar as this objective could be attained, given the complications of its religious history. But in pursuing this course, the framers of the Indian Constitution did not want to become an antireligious state any more than they wished to be a theocractic state; hence the ambiguous course of the Indian secular state in adjusting its negations to correspond with its affirmations.

Secularization as an effort to transcend religious biases and vested interests, out of concern to do justice to an entire citizenry of a culture, cannot be achieved simply by applying a theoretical definition of secularism, borrowed from another cultural history; nor can it meet the demands of an extraneous norm. It must create its own concept of secularity, keeping in mind only one controlling objective: namely, the attainment of conditions in society that will serve the well-being of its total citizenry, with a possibility of adjusting communal needs of various faiths in accordance with this larger, democratic objective. Simply to understand what is transpiring within any secular state, not to speak of assessing what is going on, one needs to keep in mind these variations in the complexity of its historical as well as its present concerns.

Given these inherent differences among secular states, can

one still establish a working definition of the concept of the secular state? I think one can if one is content with being descriptive, rather than normative; and if one is concerned simply with understanding the process of secularization, rather than with venturing prematurely upon a course of judgment.

The secular state, looked at descriptively in all its pluralistic manifestations, appears to be one that pursues a policy of providing for the physical and human well-being of the widest body of its citizenry, regardless of religious, racial, or class distinctions. To this end it concerns itself with promoting facilities, including technological, industrial, and political processes, that will assure such an inclusive state of well-being, and with regulating, or directing, the internal life of society to sustain a common sense of citizenry within the nation. Within this general description, many forms of the modern secular government have emerged, varying in temper and quality according to the conception of physical and human well-being that has been dominant and formative of national ends and means.

II

This leads us, then, to a second consideration, namely, the quality or character of life that is possible within a secular state. Governments within the modern secular state are geared to pursue rather definite social and technological objectives. In many instances, secularization has occurred rather consciously with a view to achieving these ends directly and swiftly, with an economy of psychic disturbance and obstruction. Furthermore, they are being pressed, with varying degrees of urgency, to meet the demands of this new age, but even more, to respond to opportunities being offered through new resources of power, new methods of work in science, agriculture, and industry. Yet the culture of the people, not to speak of the prevailing modes of living and working in the villages and other hinterland areas of these countries, continues to be shaped and motivated by images of existence derived from a long history of agrarian societies. Much of this heritage is obsolete; yet, in the main, it represents what still persists from the past as a summons to a qualitative outreach of the human spirit within the culture, manifest in its religions, philosophies, literature, and arts. It is here that these modern secular states run into difficulty. Secular governments, charged with the responsibility of regulating and mediating between the institutions and communal groups of societies, as these take form within the technological era, emerge as giant enterprises. As power structures, these modern governments are, at best, only remotely related to the culture of the mind and spirit expressed in the historic lore of religion, philosophy, literature, and the arts. Where the problem of harnessing and directing the new resources of power has become acute, or where national ambitions loom large, directing the nation's energies toward achieving certain sharply focused social goals, governments are led to forgo the luxury of heeding appeals from the sensitive heritage of the human spirit, represented by religion and philosophy, literature and the arts, or, for that matter, the work of the university generally. Cultures that have capitulated wholly to the demands of these new power structures, and the mode of life which they impose, have, in the main, relinquished much of their adherence to this sensitive, historical heritage. It is possible that what differentiates modern totalitarian secular states, in whatever form they may appear, from modern democratic secular states, stems from this tenuous turn of events within cultures, wherein decisions or policies of action are made either to reject or to negotiate with past values and with the institutions representing them; causing the one kind of secular government to be increasingly indifferent toward these sensitive demands in the interest of attaining the desired social goals of well-being; and the other more democratic and negotiable form to be attentive to them with varying degrees of anguish and concern, along with their drive toward technological advance.

This observation may help us to understand one major difference between types of secular states now emerging among modern cultures. Singularity of purpose in the attainment of social goals at all cost tends to evoke an open hostility to religions and traditions countering or obstructing effort toward these goals. And it may bring about a close censorship over literature and the arts as well, tolerating only such creative imagination as may advance the social purposes envisaged by government. Secularism in such governments thus implies complete disentanglement of national purposes from every historic value, save as it lends support to these immediate nationalistic ends. The secular state in this form is the nation sharply focused upon present tasks. Nationalism is its faith, and there are no other gods before it.

India and the United States have this in common, that they continue to permit the structures of critical differences within the nation to have a large degree of free play, and thus enable their secular states respectively to have access to judgments other than those devised for immediate purposes. The contrast I see between India and the United States on this issue is not one, as commonly expressed, between a spiritually motivated and a materialistically driven civilization; whatever truth may have lurked within this characterization of the two cultures originally, it no longer holds now that modern India has set its sights upon achieving improved standards of human well-being. The contrast rather, is in the nature of obstacles which each culture faces in the effort to realize the promise of its democratic form of society, and the consequent differences in governmental action, as it seeks to retain, and, at the same time, to regulate this heritage of the human spirit, expressed through religion and philosophy, literature and the arts.

There can be no doubt that you in India, through the nurture of religion, whether Hindu or Moslem, have acquired a facility for corporate living that makes individual freedom in the new situation, or even the demand for it, a persisting problem. Conversely, it must be said, that we in the United States, having been nurtured in a tradition of individualism, born of religious and political revolt, have acquired a bent toward individual freedom that renders all demands for corporate responsibility troublesome, if not offensive. Our religion and philosophy, art and literature, tend to elevate this audacity of the individual, and to accentuate the demand for it; though the circumstances being created by the new structures of power compel us to be more responsive to the commonweal. You most certainly have within your philosophical tradition the appeal to the authentic self, and the disciplines by which it is nurtured. In fact, our American philosopher, Ralph Waldo Emerson, the poet of self-reliance who has taught us much, learned much in turn from your seers. Yet the faiths and the religious communities with which your modern secular state must deal has provided a different kind of nurture, one that intensified the communal character of living and its dependencies. Thus the problem that is made acute in your situation as a secular state is precisely that of addressing the individual as citizen, independently of religion or caste, while our most acute problem in the United States tends to be that of transcending self-interest in deference to corporate demands that are real and imperative. I do not mean that we do not transcend them, or that we do not have a large reserve of generosity and social good will; any more than I mean to say that you in India do not have a significant degree of individuality and independence of spirit, and respect for the individual. I am speaking here solely of the prevailing cultural circumstances that confront the government of the secular state in each instance, and which thus present problems of a different order, modifying to some extent the form of secularity in government that is evoked and exercised, and thus modifying also the concept of the secular state in our respective cultures. Granting these distinctions between us, it is nevertheless true that on the crucial issue to which we have been addressing ourselves, the relations between persisting cultural sensibilities and immediate goals, we are more alike than different. In short, we may say that in India, as in the United States, the protest and tempering of its spiritual heritage continues to restrain and influence its material ambitions. It is this that distinguishes the secular state among liberal democracies from the secularism of totalitarian cultures.

III

I turn now to the third and final aspect of our discussion of the secular state. So far we have tried to avoid bringing a normative measure to bear upon our study of the modern secular state in the interest of ackowledging its many facets with their complexity. Eventually, however, anyone who is concerned with the total life of man within any culture as an expression of the larger life of the human spirit will be compelled to come to some judgments about the contemporary processes of secularization as they appear in modern states. For example, he will be led to ask, after observing certain concrete examples in present history, Is secularization, in its drive toward physical and human well-being, always destined to become a self-conscious truncation of man's existence in deference to practical demands? In other

words, must this legacy of imaginative and spiritual creativity be ignored or rejected in order to achieve these more
practical ends? Does it necessarily lead to the suppression of
individual creativity, or of corporate differences of interest
and commitment within the culture? Does it focus attention
exclusively upon immediate nationalistic demands to the exclusion of ultimate concerns, or more basic principles of existence with which sensitive and religiously minded members of the community are normally concerned? These are
some of the questions which arise when one considers the
secular state as a cultural phenomenon affecting the life of
the community as a whole, or in its ultimate aspect.

One may be helped toward reaching some judgment concerning these questions in two ways: One way is to look at
the working definition of the secular state, insofar as it is
definable. Our discussion so far has raised some questions
about this procedure; but there is insight to be gained
through pursuing it for a moment. Considering this procedure, one may say that it will make a difference if the establishment of the secular state follows from a concern with
the well-being of a people together with some appreciation
of the dimension of man's existence to which agencies of society other than government minister. This more measured
effort to create a margin of secularity within the culture
without categorically subjecting all other aspects of its life
to this intention will lead to a conception of the secular state
as being instrumental, rather than constitutive. The secular
state, so conceived, despite its economic power and necessary interference in the processes of life, will assume the role
of servant to the larger good of society, and will be regarded
as the agent of the people in the full sense of the term. Legislative acts will be representative of an electorate provided
by the people. This will imply a certain capacity on the part
of individual members of a community to transcend reli-

gious and intellectual interests to some extent, insofar as they represent individual commitments, in behalf of, or in deference to, negotiable acts with other members of the community, looking to the welfare and the critical demands of immediacies for all. Where such voluntary negotiation is not forthcoming in a society, the secular state, even as the representative of the people, will be compelled to become coercive, though this will be an expedient, rather than a customary form of action.

A secular state, on the other hand, that conceives of itself as being expressive of substantive ends, in defiance of all contrary concerns, or as being a revolutionary change in the culture so radical and deep as to imply a repudiation of that culture's history, and of the sensibilities consonant with its traditions, will bring to the very meaning of the secular state a more singular and narrowing understanding of its objectives. Clearly it will not be a negotiable agency within the culture, or a servant of a representative will of the people. It will not wait on voluntary motivation, education, or commitment, but will proceed coercively in exercising the power it has attained, or seized.

By definition, then, one will see that the concept of the secular state itself provides an answer to the questions raised concerning the total life of the culture, seen historically or contemporaneously. In the one instance, all the questions remain open, depending upon degrees of flexibility, intelligence, and negotiability that are made possible within its citizenry. The concrete experiences of government and people themselves hold the key to these answers, whether the secular state will mean the truncation of the nation's life, whether it will lead to the suppression of individual creativity and of corporate differences, whether it will compel all the processes of the culture to capitulate to nationalistic drives to the exclusion of all transcending visions of whatever kind. The situation is quite otherwise in a secular state bent upon totalitarian ends. Here the very concept of the secular state carries within itself the necessity of answering each of these questions in a doctrinaire fashion. It will be led to decree that, of course secularization must mean a truncation of the cultural life, holding it to proportions made manageable by its defined objectives, and sloughing off all else as a needless threat to those objectives. It will hold that of course secularization in such a state must mean the suppression of individual creativity, and the replacement of it with a corporate creativity that can be more controllable, and to which individual talent and imagination is to be made subservient. It will decree that corporate differences must be suppressed, and the interchange of ideas closely guarded and frequently censored, lest reflection and the expression of ideas get out of hand and become obstructive to the defined objectives. Such a conception of the secular state must produce aggressive nationalism, or its counterpart in a particularistic internationalism. And there can be no concessions to any other competing or associated ends.

A second way by which one may be helped toward reaching some judgment concerning the questions raised, is to look at concrete instances of secularization in the modern state. We will confine ourselves here to the secular state among the democracies. We saw that by definition of the concept of the secular state, the questions concerning the cultural effects of secularization remained open. The flexible, negotiable character of its secularity gave promise of escaping or of overcoming the conditions cited. While the course of culture is not assured in such a secular state, the restraints of inherited sensibilities, or concerns consonant with ideals of human freedom, may be appealed to; critical and prophetic voices from any source, challenging governmental policy or action, are free to be heard; and, because they can speak through representative bodies or agencies, they may be listened to, and thus be made effective as reform and legislative influences within the culture.

The open society thus carries within its own routine practices, the checks and balances to guide the secular state toward humane and humanistic ends, even as it serves the physical well-being of its people.

Yet the actual circumstances within each of these democratic cultures, following from their secularizing intentions, do present problems which are as perplexing as they are persisting. And here I must recount some occurrences within both the Indian and the American experience which bring out the more dire aspect of the democratic secular state. You will know the concrete circumstances in India giving substance to this assertion. To an outsider, simply observing the public life of Indian cities and communities, the secular state in India appears to be grappling with almost unmanageable problems. While it presumes to be open to the appeals of all faiths within the nation, and concerned to negotiate tensions or difficulties which will inevitably arise in any society, it finds itself historically and currently involved in the affairs of the Hindu community in a way that it is not bound to any other religious group. Despite the effort of government representatives to deal objectively with this situation, or to steer a secular course, the undertow and overtones of involvement plague its every effort to transcend these problems.

Again, India struggles with problems of inefficiency and lack of integrity in its civil service that place an almost insuperable burden upon a secular government seeking to remain within the ethos of a democracy. One Indian resident who had lived in India most of her mature years said, "When one cannot mail a letter without concern about the stamp being removed or stolen, or check one's train bag-

gage without worrying about its being pilfered, or seek the
help of police or the courts with some assurance of fair
treatment at their hands without resorting to bribery, the
sheer act of living out each day becomes too arduous to be
tolerated." To secular states concerned to remain within the
democratic-socialistic frame of government, it is disconcert-
ing to have it observed that totalitarian states have been able
to cope decisively with such blatant civil offenses. They are
able to do so, of course, because of the authoritarian arm
that reaches from its centralized control into every department of government, and into every community within the
nation. It is significant, and somewhat disturbing, that sensitive Indian citizens, distressed over the many nuisances, ab-
surdities, and corrupt practices which one must put up with
in dealing with post offices, railroads, courts, and police
headquarters in modern India, have cited modern China
or even Pakistan as examples of what can be done to rid
modern society of corruption in its civil service.[9] "Neither
communism nor a culture controlled by religious laws," I
heard one Indian say, "would tolerate what we have to put
up with in India in the running of our post offices, courts,
and law enforcement agencies."

Much is overlooked in this blanket acclaim of totalitarian
states as a cure-all for a corrupt civil service; but it does un-
derscore the desperateness with which Indian citizens view
the unwieldy character of the cultural situation in transition
in a democratic, secular state. Where power is distributed,
yet vested in bureaucratic agencies, individuals or groups of
citizens are in a position to exploit their fellow men for self-
ish ends. One of the complaints frequently overheard among

[9] Recent news accounts of corruption in Pakistan's civil service indicate
that totalitarian control, even when directed by religious norms and traditions, offers no guarantee against such a breakdown in a nation's civil
service.

sensitive and pubic-spirited Indians is that India's independence has engulfed Indian communities in an endless sea of exploitation at the hands of their own countrymen. Said one Indian banker, distraught over what he had been experiencing in his community, "When one of our countrymen seizes power or receives it through appointment or election, the only way he knows how to use it is to exploit his fellow Indians." Whether this kind of remark is but a cynical overstatement, or a telling observation, an outside observer will be hesitant to judge, but again, it voices a despair with the exercise of civil authority in a democratic society that must evoke serious concern.

This situation poses a problem that strikes at the very heart of the secular state in a democratic society; for with its wide distribution of power, direction and control of the various branches of government are difficult to achieve or to sustain. For these must depend to a large extent upon the moral motivation of its citizenry, expressing itself through its representative individuals or agencies. And the extent to which such motivation can be evoked and implemented will depend upon the degree to which individual and corporate responsibility for the commonweal is felt and acknowledged. Democracy demands such internal motivation, else it disintegrates into a power struggle between petty clusters of self-interested groups, employing the freedom of the political processes to exploit opportunities for partisan ends. This is a problem we know well in the United States. With active lobbying groups pressuring our elected representatives in government to serve their partisan ends through legislative acts, our American democracy is threatened with becoming just an interplay of power groups, except as a more public spirited motivation, looking to the larger ends of the corporate life, succeeds in restraining or re-directing these partisan drives. Evoking and sustaining such motivation in a secular state is not impossible, but the obstacles to achieving it are numerous and persistent.

Yet my own knowledge of life in the United States leads me to realize that the problems attending the secular state among democracies, however well motivated, are grave and disturbing for other reasons. The sheer absorption of time and energy among members of legislative, judicial, and executive branches of our government in making decisions bearing upon the practical demands of the nation's business crowds out much that could otherwise be noted or contemplated, were decisions to proceed directly from first principles, delivered by fiat or by tradition from some transcendent source. This situation is due to the complexity of the deliberative process itself. A secular state within a liberal democracy is almost by nature destined to become a business civilization by the character of its political process, and by the concern to keep it attuned to the will of the people. And because these interests have such a commanding voice, they become determinative of much else within the culture as well. They become major activities in a sense which no other cultural activities or interests can emulate. Education, religion, the arts, these are important enough in their own spheres, or possibly as appendages to the life of business and industry; but they are not commanding sources of judgment and action. This is a tendency that is difficult to avoid in a secular state among the democracies. It is no accident therefore that the United States of America has become known as a business civilization, implying a secondary role for all other activities in its culture. It is not a destiny that was intended. Men of culture, deeply sensitive in their religious and moral concerns, some of them gifted as men of letters, have shaped and guided our ship of state. Taken individually, many of them were among the West's most scholarly and gifted human beings. And individually they cherished the things of the spirit. But a culture governed by a secular state is not necessarily the lengthened shadow of the men who guide it. There is an impersonal equation that tends to loom persuasively and, in time, to assume a sovereign hold upon the culture's values. This is a menacing aspect of the secular state within democracies that cannot be gainsaid. Perhaps the experiment in which India is now engaged will prove significant in proportion as it learns to grapple with this tendency inherent within the secular state. You have a momentum of spiritual concern, a legacy of literary and artistic achievement, together with a sensitive style of living within corporate patterns of life that give depths of quality and aspiration to your cultural experiences. These are not yours alone; for they have been conveyed directly or indirectly to many of the world's people, and they are cherished as a gift of your own peculiar heritage. So much of the human spirit in its noblest creation is symbolized by what you have explicitly said as a people, as well as by what you have exemplified as human beings. I need not recount names to you, but three of them of the modern period have become symbols of humanity at high tide for people of all nations: Rabindranath Tagore, Mahatma Gandhi, and Jawaharlal Nehru. The range of power and spiritual attainment represented by these three human beings of your culture spans the spectrum of human creativity. In diverse ways they express the fulfillment of the human venture at its maximum. That your experiment in establishing a secular state should have had men of this stature guiding and shaping its course in its initial stages, is a privilege no other modern nation, in my judgment, has shared. Surely more than the usual mixture of men and machines should be forthcoming from the years of travail and triumph through which these dedicated men led your people. But I repeat here what I observed earlier: a secular state is not necessarily the lengthened shadow of the men who have guided it. There are stubborn processes extending beyond the human dimension of personality, requiring attention, and thereby, as history too often has indicated, demanding acquiescence as well. It is this delicate balance that can turn the tide of a culture's experience, either in the direction of full capitulation to the problems and demands of physical well-being, or in a direction that can summon these structures of society to be responsive, even answerable, to more sensitive demands of the human spirit.

Furthermore, the success in sustaining either efficiency or a human quality of life within a democratic secular society hinges perilously upon there being a substantial margin of integrity in the processes of government as well as in the electorate. No democratic society can maintain itself without a working degree of integrity at all levels of its operations. For reasons that you and I know only too well, this poses a serious problem for all secular democratic states.

The potentiality of India's conquest of these issues has been great, but it is not yet assured. On the outcome of this conquest rests the destiny of India's national life and more. And this *more* that awaits it could be exhilarating beyond any words to express it. It would be so were it not accompanied by undertones of despair, expressive of the historical anguish of older experiments in Europe and in the United States, wherein an aroused humanity, defiant of this age of machines and its secularity, cries out against its dehumanization of man, and against its ultimate absurdity. It would be so were it not accompanied by undertones of skepticism and misgiving within the Indian people themselves as they witness a deterioration in the processes of government, aggravated by corruption and a cynical acceptance of its inevitable occurrence in a democratic society.

Nevertheless, India stands within a second era of liberalism, a second era of hope and energy, grappling with machines as agencies and instruments of hope for a people in need of the sustenance they can provide; grappling, too, against seemingly overwhelming odds, with an unrelenting self-interest that pervades every democratic society, corroding the spirit of man and his community of interests as a human society. All this to assure men some material gain. With food for the body assured, will the spirit survive? This is the crucial question. It is, in fact, the question being posed to every modern secular state.

Secularization Arising from Science and Technology

Science and technology present a common set of problems to modern cultures wherever industrialization is in progress. This has not always been true; for science and technology have not always been as closely allied in their operations as they are today. In an informative study entitled *The Scientific Revolution and World Politics*, Dr. Caryl P. Haskins, President of the Carnegie Institution of Washington, distinguishes between the historical development of technology and the rise of modern science. Technology, he points out, has an older history. Its roots go back some three thousand years to the growth of cities in Egypt, Mesopotamia, Babylon, and North India, when "men lived in cities at least as well planned and serviced as many of their counterparts in the same region today."[1] The scientific revolution in the West, culminating in the Newtonian era, arose independently of this earlier technological history, and remained aloof from such developments until a generation after

[1] Haskins, Caryl P., *The Scientific Revolution and World Politics*, New York: Harper & Row, 1964, p. 30.

Newton, when industrialization in England began. In its earlier stages, says Haskins, the scientific revolution in the West was almost wholly concerned with problems relating to the nature of the physical universe. In the language of academic circles, it was committed to inquiries in pure science, in contrast to the practical concerns of technology. Isaac Newton referred to his own investigations as "natural philosophy," which is suggestive of the sphere and scope of his scientific inquiry. It can be said, too, that the revolution that the sciences initiated in the West was one that affected man's image of himself and his world, and thus had to do chiefly with fundamental notions by which man's understanding of the natural world could be formulated. To be sure, there were instances of technological development during the earlier stages of European science, such as da Vinci's numerous experiments, and developments in the Italian city states; yet, prior to the industrial era in the West, developments in technology were sporadic and intermittent. Its major developments in the West belong to the modern world, more particularly to the recent period following from the correlation of scientific and industrial efforts. In the United States one sees a beginning of this correlation in the so-called "invention factories" which were developed under Thomas Edison in the nineteenth century and later. Here scientific genius was applied to inventive purposes on a mass scale. In time it was to be incorporated into industry as a necessary aspect of its own developing enterprise. The employment of scientists by industry has now become an accepted and commonplace fact. The affiliation between industry and university centers of research, and between government and university research centers, are of more recent origin, and express a growing interdependence between science and technology. This latter phase, leading to large-scale developments in technology, belongs to the period dating from the last World War, when nuclear science became an explicit and public area of research.

Today science and technology seem inseparable. With the need of bringing scientific research into the employ of governments, the correlation has become even more intimate and binding, until scientists themselves have had reason to wonder if scientific inquiry, as an independent and universal discipline, is any longer possible, or can ever be reestablished as it was known prior to the nuclear age, before governments took an active and proprietary interest in it. A moving account of this changing scientific scene is given by James B. Conant in a book entitled *Modern Science and Modern Man*, published in 1952. This situation is accentuated in totalitarian states where scientific research is explicitly directed by governmental needs and policies. But even in the democracies, the governmental control of science in the interest of technological advance, either for military or civil ends, cannot be wholly abandoned, however much mitigated by policies and devices to keep research free and independent. So much, then, for the general history of our problem.

I

In what I am about to say about the secularizing effects following from the correlation of science and technology, I am presupposing that their impact upon modern cultures is world wide in scope. This assumption has not always been made in discussions of science and cultural affairs. For almost three hundred years interpreters of this problem have tended to assume that issues between science and religion, or between industrialization and spiritual values, were preoccupations of the West. We have been led to assume, even by some of your own Eastern interpreters that scientific thinking is an alien mode of thought to the East, and that industrialization is foreign to its way of doing things. Undoubtedly, certain stereotypes, passing for images distinguishing the cultures of the East from those of the West, have followed from these assumptions, many of which have been misleading, or simply false. To a degree, of course, these characterizations are apt and indicative of our different histories. Professor Haskins has observed, for example, that Asia remained relatively untouched by the scientific revolution following from Newton. It is true that scholars in the East were familiar with these scientific notions following from the scientific revolution, and through these scholars the scientific thinking of the West became common knowledge to anyone in the East concerned to study them or to make them his own. But the scientific revolution of this earlier period did not, he argues, affect *the cultural thinking of the East as a whole* in the way that it reshaped much of Western thinking following Newton's time. And it was these "years following Newton . . . that constituted the general revolution when the visions that had earlier compelled the pioneers (such as Copernicus and Galileo) *suddenly infected a much wider public*." This is the important point to keep in mind here. "It is hard indeed at this distance," Haskins continues, "to appreciate fully the incandescence of the Newtonian revolution when it captured the imagination of a whole people."[2]

However valid it may have been a generation or more ago to set the West apart from the East in its encounter with science and technology, the notion that these disciplines and technical processes are alien to Asian thinking and life is no longer tenable, and has not been since the emergence of the modern era, particularly since the formation of the new nations in the East, beginning in the 1940's.

[2] Ibid. p. 42.

It can be argued, however, that the new nations have experienced more of the impact of technology than of modern science in the cultural revolutions that have been occurring. Modern China appears to be somewhat of an exception in this regard in its recent efforts to come to terms with nuclear science. The picture here is not easily brought into focus, principally because we have not had direct access to what has been occurring during the past two decades among Chinese scientists. Says Dr. Haskins,

No American scientist has visited China to witness its technology and its science at first hand since the regime of Mao who came to power in 1949. From that time until 1958 there had probably been less than a score of visitors from Britain and even fewer from other of the free nations of Europe, and there had been virtually no formal and discerning accounts of Chinese science and technology. The bamboo curtain has been equally opaque from the other side. Communist China has resolutely declined invitations to join the International Council of Scientific Unions—because of the membership of Taiwan in that body—and scientific representatives from the "Peoples Republic" have been conspicuously absent at all the conferences sponsored by the Council and from related international contacts.[3]

Despite this lack of what Dr. Haskins calls "hard information," relevant firsthand data has become available; and from this data, "an extensive body of highly informed inference" has been distilled. On the basis of such data and inference, Dr. Haskins comes to the conclusion that "Chinese technology and Chinese science are impressive today, and they are rapidly becoming more so."[4]

This was supposed even before the news of China's nuclear testing was disclosed. Now it is clear at least that some basic scientific research has been possible and is at present in

[3] Ibid. p. 91.
[4] Ibid. p. 92.

progress among Chinese scientists. And this adds a new dimension of concern to what was already known about its technology efforts.[5]

In the book just quoted, Dr. Haskins also surveys the programs being projected in various new nations, such as Saudi Arabia, Turkey, Pakistan, India, and Indonesia, and finds "in many respects the most interesting and the most critical phases of the scientific revolutions" are occurring here.

Such nations, located particularly in Eastern Europe, along the Mediterranean littoral, in the Near and Middle East, on the Indian Peninsula, and in parts of Southeast Asia and South America, are already culturally integral parts of the modern world, with essentially modern views of the whole scientific "style" of the universe.[6]

He finds India particularly active in basic research and inquiry in the area of food production, including agronomy and crop and animal improvement and soil science.[7]

"India," he says, "is outstanding . . . in the number and variety of her research and technological institutions, among them many devoted wholly or in part to problems of food production. . . . Probably no one of the developing countries at the lower economic levels possesses so great a potential to determine immediate relevances in specific technologies."[8]

These observations, to be sure, reflect a close correlation of basic science with technological needs. And this is a pattern that tends to prevail throughout modern cultures, suggesting that concern with the practical consequences of

[5] A more specific analysis of the current nuclear situation in modern China has appeared in Morton H. Halperin, *China and the Bomb*, New York: Praeger, 1965.
[6] Ibid. pp. 49-50.
[7] Ibid. pp. 18-19.
[8] Ibid. p. 19.

the sciences is more in focus among modern nations than the probing being undertaken in basic research. And this tendency could mean, in turn, that the effects of the sciences in correlation with technology upon these new cultures are to be discerned more in their changing mode of existence than in the more abstract areas of thought.

This brings us to the general observation that the acute problems of secularization in present-day cultures, stemming from science and industry, are of a kind that issue from this intimate correlation of science and technology, affecting, not so much presuppositions in thought, as the conditions of men's lives and the tastes and sensibilities they develop in response to these new conditions. This stands in sharp contrast to the situation in the West during its early history. The earliest impact of the sciences upon Western culture took the form of *secularizing thought,* of setting up, as formative notions, conceptions of the world and of man which were alien to its inherited ethos, which in this case was the Judaic-Christian tradition. Scientific theories in that climate of thought stood opposed to Biblical views of creation. Scientific principles of causation ruled out the religious teaching concerning miracles, or the supernatural work of grace. A scientific world view, so it appeared to scientifically minded people of that generation, left no room for a belief in Providence, or for the intervention of a transcendent God in the events of history. This was the secularizing influence of *pure science* upon Western thinking, as it was translated into "natural philosophy," before the correlation of science and technology had made its impact upon modern societies.

I do not mean to speak of this earlier form of secularization wholly as an historical problem. It persists as acutely as ever in many places, particularly in the United States. And many of the same problems that disturbed nineteenth-century thinking in the West continue to evoke spirited reaction and resistance in these areas of our culture. However, with the emergence of a new vision of science, following from discoveries and reformulations in modern physics, the situation has radically changed in the more sophisticated areas of our thought. As a result, the scientific outlook in the West, especially among critical minds who have more acquaintance with relativity physics and quantum theory, is not the threat to ultimate religious notions of man and his world that it was in the years following Newton and Darwin.

From conversations I have had with some of your scholars and educators, I would judge that something of this kind of response to the sciences is to be found in India as well. Some years ago, during an earlier visit to your country, I had extensive conversations with several men in your universities and colleges. An Indian historian in one of the colleges in north India was particularly disturbed by what he saw developing in Indian schools. Being a devout Hindu, he was concerned over the fact that the teaching of scientific studies was increasing in Indian schools, even at the level of village education. What disturbed him most about the teaching of the sciences in the schools was its alien character as a discipline. In the case of literature, art, history, even philosophy, he said, students are studying something that has continuity with traditions of thought that were familiar to them in childhood, when they shared in the culture of the hearth, hearing the stories and legends of India's past as they were related by a great aunt or grandmother. The humanistic studies, he said, are simply this culture of antiquity more fully explored, analyzed, and interpreted. They may create a more mature response to this religious legacy, a different rationale for holding to its vision of life, yet they nevertheless remain within an orbit of meaning that is conversant with that heritage. With the sciences, he observed, the case is quite different. What do any of them have to do with the Vedas or the Bhagavad Gita, or any other portion of our literature? They require a sharp detour of the mind from all that this heritage represents, and when the student takes up with this kind of study (and they do, as you know, with great relish in our college, he remarked parenthetically) he becomes a divided person, or he loses contact altogether with what he has known as part of the family heritage.

This response to science in your culture expresses anxieties over a kind of secularization that is comparable to that which elicited concern among Christians of the West in the post-Newtonian and Darwinian eras. I would not say there are no grounds for this concern, but, in retrospect, I am persuaded that the secularization envisaged here is not as serious a threat to the life of the spirit in a culture as other, more recent forms accompanying the technological era. As has been discovered in the West, the impact of the sciences upon traditional views of man and his world can stimulate critical inquiry into the religious mores and beliefs, not necessarily with the result of dissolving them or dismissing them, but with the effect of summoning them to a more discerning level of understanding and commitment. A critical sense in religious thought can be both purgative and revitalizing, stripping its over-burdened tradition of expendable over-beliefs, yet wresting from the critical interchange with the sciences a firmer hold on what constitutes the substance of one's ultimate faith.

But it is also true that the winds of doctrine within the sciences change, so that, whereas scientific judgment in one era may effect a denial of the claims of faith, new discoveries or reformulations in a later period may rescind or so modify former scientific views as to open up new dimensions of inquiry in which both science and religion are able to come into a fuller vision of man's meaning and his understanding of his world. This has been the story of the encounter between science and religion in Western history during the past century,[9] though I must hasten to say that a commitment to one's past religious legacy that envisages no change, or that resists all modification in deference to modern times, has every reason to fear the incursion of the sciences. For science is a disrupting force among rigid orthodoxies; and it brooks no closure of the mind with patience or consideration. Its spirit is one of ruthless integrity, bent on inquiry into whatever will yield to its probing, penetrating procedures.

The problem of dealing with the issues that arise out of conflicting world-views, out of clashes between the sacred lore of Scripture and the findings of the sciences is, I repeat, a serious one wherever it is encountered. And there is anguish of mind and spirit in confronting the tensions that arise within a culture where these issues intrude. But the problems it raises are not insurmountable. And the outcome of meeting them can be an advance in the educational and religious outlook of a people. In this sense the secularization which the sciences can bring to a culture, with all its iconoclasm and controversy, is more in the nature of a challenge to traditional values than a fatal threat to them.

II

But now I invite you to look at a more subtle aspect of this problem. A more serious form of secularization than the one we have been considering may follow from the indirect impact of scientific discovery and experimentation upon a

[9] See Harold K. Schilling, *Science and Religion*, New York: Scribner's, 1962. See also B. E. Meland, *Realities of Faith*, New York: Oxford University Press, 1962, Part I.

culture. Although traditional images of man and his world may persist in a culture side by side with scientific theories, the day-to-day work of the sciences and of technology today proceeds without benefit of these overtones of ultimate meanings, and with habitual indifference to them. While in Newton's time scientific research could presuppose an ultimate cosmic order underlying the piecemeal efforts of scientists to inquire into its processes, the nuclear scientist today is apt to regard all such ultimate notions as being unavailable to him, except as he chooses to affirm them as over-beliefs, as an act of faith. There are scientists of stature who, like the late Albert Einstein,[10] insist upon holding to a vision of ultimate orderliness as a necessary presupposition of scientific inquiry, even though they share in the post-Newtonian judgment that scientific theorems can no longer be regarded as "picture models"[11] of these natural processes. Many laboratory scientists and technicians, however, tend to eschew such overbeliefs; or assume that there is nothing beyond the humdrum routine of the laboratory. This change in attitude toward an ultimate conception of orderliness in the universe imposes upon the scientific discipline itself a restrictive view of scientific labors which has cultural consequences beyond these labors themselves. One may put it this way: In a culture in which a world-order is imagined or affirmed, the life-order of a people is thought to be consonant with it, or in some sense a response to it. When the notion of a world-order vanishes, the only order that remains is what Karl Jaspers has called the "life-order"—that is, the accepted rhythm of routine

[10] See Paul Schilpp (ed.), *Albert Einstein: Philosopher Scientist,* New York: Tudor, 1941, p. 176. See discussion of this point in Albert William Levi, *Philosophy and the Modern World,* Indiana University Press, 1959, p. 265f. and in B. E. Meland, op. cit. pp. 150ff.
[11] Ian T. Ramsey's phrase, in *Models and Mystery,* London: Oxford University Press, 1964.

activities and of objectives which serve an accepted purpose in society. Such a life-order may have no reference or meaning beyond the functions that are exercised, or the immediate satisfactions that are met. Man thus simply exists within these routine activities, and for them.

The technological era created and sustained by science and industry can be described as such a life-order, expressive not only of the day-to-day activity of those who work in laboratories and factories, but of the mode of life among many of their contemporaries for whom these routine activities determine and limit their understanding of existence. This, as you can see, stands in sharp contrast to earlier periods of our history, even among scientists themselves. At that time, as we have noted, both scientists and industrialists were answerable to or responsible to what was assumed to be a world-order. Thus participation in their activities was to some degree participation in the principles, laws, and ethos of this larger image of life. What distinguishes much of modern life, rooted in the activities of science and industry, from previous periods of history is the dissociation of these workaday efforts from the notion of an ultimate cosmic order underlying all such activities.

Although scientists diverge on this basic issue of an ultimate Order, as we have said, the men who work in laboratories on specific projects, especially when they are engaged in projects allied with industry, think and move within a sphere of knowledge and purpose which is expressive of immediate cycles of cause and effect, and nothing more. Thus their movements and decisions are dictated by judgments that express no other order of meaning except those of immediate functions and ends. In this sense, science and industry constitute in themselves secular orders of activities. That is, they neither presuppose nor address themselves to any ultimate end, or order of meaning, nor do they serve to inform or nurture concern with such ends. You will note that I am depicting here an influential strand of scientific thinking—not the outlook of all scientists.

Thus, when science and technology are translated into a life-order that is communicable beyond the laboratory, they become agencies of a more formidable kind of secularization than anything that has thus far come forth from modern history, more serious in its threat to religious sensibilities in my judgment than the scientific naturalism of the nineteenth century and after. It is so because it is more encompassing of life itself in communities, and more rigorous in what it sets forth as a commentary upon the life processes in which all men of the culture share. Science is then thought to hold all the answers to men's problems. And in this role it becomes a new Messiah.

III

There is yet a further sense in which science and technology contribute to the making of a secularized life-order. What renders science and technology so vulnerable as purveyors of secularization in any culture is the impersonal and abstract character of the processes upon which they depend and which they employ. Living realities are reduced to pin points and to statistical equations. A vast array of graphs and figures forms the faceless portrait of statistical man. The mass effect, generalities writ large, are what survive and determine decisions.

We should not fail to recognize the beneficent strand of meaning that runs through this maze of abstractions and mass effort. What lifts the level of human well-being for each individual in a technological society is the accumulation of highly specialized knowledge and its application to human need. Science and technology contribute this to mankind! Yet in this statistical measure, individual values or

concerns centering in minority interests, which may represent something of high quality or some peculiar need, tend
to be obscured or lost sight of. Furthermore, we would be
most sanguine and naïve if we were to assume that the
knowledge and resources that come to hand from such
statistical study are put to service only to improve our human condition and to minister to human need.

In a technological society promotion and enterprise become a necessity, and the means at hand, often subtle and
concealed, can be highly effective in directing and controlling public opinion or consumer judgment. In all of this,
man is a utility, a point on the chart, or a puppet to be
manipulated for ulterior ends. It is both the overt use of
these resources of abstract knowledge and data for dubious
and even for corrupt ends, as well as their consequent effects upon the human psyche, that contribute to the pathology we have called secularization. Both the dignity and the
spiritual stature of the human spirit are at stake in this issue.
Both the meaning and identity of man as man, and each
man's own self-understanding and esteem, are involved here.

But even the good that is served by such technical skill
and its resources can contribute to decadence in a technological society. For an economy of abundance is put to it
to remain fluid and productive. Hence consumption must
keep pace with production. This endless cycle of necessity
accentuates the concern with marketable goods and the need
for more and more of them in numerous varieties until
"things really are in the saddle and ride mankind." Man's
sense of need is elastic and can be made to respond to stim-
ulation. There is literally no end to which this concern with
creature comfort or appetition and its ministries can be carried in a technological society. This, in fact, becomes all-
absorbing because it is so basic to the survival of the structure of life that promotes it. Thus a structural necessity and

a cultivated sense of need combine to lift secondary themes of existence to a major preoccupation. Physical comfort and well-being become the all-important goals of man's life. Accordingly, man's sense of dependence upon trivial discrimination in every aspect of his physical well-being increases. The sheer expenditure of time and energy in satisfying these cultivated needs can be enormous. The days and the years will not suffice to encompass them. We are familiar with the kind of human degradation that results from poverty and from the lack of proper and adequate means to heal and nurture the body; but there is also human degradation that follows from the pursuit of physical well-being when this is made the chief and all-absorbing end of life.

The problem of attaining physical well-being among the peoples of the world has become so acute and central in the struggles of world revolution today that no one can simply dismiss this concern as being a symptom of secularization. For in confronting the fact that pathologies do occur and have occurred in our own exaggerated pursuit of this end, we cannot be oblivious of the haunting fact that millions of human beings are being denied their humanity for lack of a concern with well-being. Yet it does give one pause to realize that, in transmitting one's own cultural experience in scientific invention and industry to other cultures in need of bodily renewal, one may also be transmitting the pathologies that accompany this concern as well.

Summarizing our observations, then, we may say that the secularization of life contributed by science and industry through technology to any culture is seen to assume three aspects: (1) the secularization of processes within the scientific discipline itself and its activities; (2) the secularization of the processes of thought with which social issues and other public problems are approached and analyzed; and

(3) the secularization of the image of man through statistical methods, and their application in the concern with mass production and mass marketing. Secularization in this last instance results in something more debasing than the trivializing of man's image of himself; it reaches the human psyche with debilitating effects, leveling down the qualitative outreach of man to the point where incentive to growth, discipline, and refinement of sensibility is arrested, as the egoistic demands of undisciplined tastes assume ascendancy.

The very presence and persistence of this secularized sphere of significant workaday activity, yielding up knowledge, resources, and directives of increasing magnitude and stature, has a telling effect upon the culture itself. And in an age in which science and technology tend to assume increasing prestige as being indispensable to the culture's security and sustenance, while the more humanistic and religious aspects of its life are made voluntary or optional interests of the individual, or are even looked upon by some as being expendable, the total effect of this secularizing influence can be decisive. The culture as a whole then comes to conceive of itself as being beholden to this highly significant sphere of secular thought and activity in a way that it would not ascribe dependence to religious sensibilities, philosophical wonder and reflection, or aesthetic satisfaction and judgment.

The secularizing of life in the sense in which we have been speaking has proceeded farther in the West than in the East, though the momentum in this direction is accelerating among some cultures of the East. And the indications are clear that the pressure of revolutionary demands now operative will further accelerate these secularizing processes.

But now I must add a word of warning: let no one take these remarks to be an endorsement of indiscriminate blasts against science and technology, or to be an expression only of criticism of these impressive areas of modern achievement. The indebtedness of modern man to science and technology is beyond measure. And the extent of the contributions they may yet make to human society is unimaginable, even within the limited spheres now known to us.

But it is no service to the sciences, or to humankind, to ignore or to suppress evidence of pathologies being transmitted to human living, even by the best of our disciplined achievements. It is, in fact, the counsel of scientists themselves that has been most insistent in alerting us to these dangers, and on preparing us to enter into this new age of science and technology with our eyes open, and with our critical judgment awakened, knowing that, for all its wonder and fascination, the way that is being opened up before us is a precarious one, a way fraught with issues that speak of life and death for all mankind. Nothing short of our best intelligence, and the courage to be candid in facing its realities, will serve us and our fellowmen in this precarious and historic hour of our destiny.

To this warning, I should like to add a note of hope. Inasmuch as science and technology have commended themselves to the new nations as agencies of renewal, providing resources and facilities for lifting the level of human livelihood, it is quite likely that they may find ways to assimilate these new enterprises without necessarily incurring some of the cultural consequences that have been noted in the West. Wherever there is the possibility for new alternatives to past experience, there can be hope that a better solution to human problems may be forthcoming. In this sense, we of the West look to the East with some expectancy in their present encounter with science and technology.

These remarks of mine recall a conversation which took place some years ago between one of your scientists and one of ours. The American physicist, the late Arthur Compton, told of a meeting with the Indian scientist, Sir Shanti Bhanagar. They were talking of the future of India, and Sir Shanti turned to Professor Compton, saying, "There is one thing that you in the West can teach us in the East. It is something that matters tremendously. Show us that it is good to live in an industrialized community."[12]

With a strange ironical twist in the events of history, we in the West now find ourselves addressing this very same plea to the people of the new nations, who, as it were, represent a second chance in the history of modern civilization to assimilate science and technology to the culture of the human spirit. Show us that it really can be good to live in a technological society!

[12] Quoted in C. A. Coulson, *Science, Technology and the Christian*, New York: Abingdon Press, 1960, p. 104.

The Dissolution of Historical Sensibilities

Secularization in modern times appears purposeful and inescapable in the conscious efforts of present-day governments and of some political agencies to restrain or to control religions in the interest of national advance toward social goals. Thus we were led earlier to look upon the secular state in modern cultures, at least in certain significant instances, as contributing constructively to the issues of existence that are before us in the present age. Here we are to consider a form of secularization in modern times in which the spiritual dimension of man appears to be more flagrantly challenged, and possibly more seriously threatened. I have called this form of secularization the dissolution of historical sensibilities. This is an old theme. Every generation, both ancient and modern, has provided its variations upon this theme. At its most superficial level it is simply the revolt of youth against their intolerable forebears; or, perhaps, the anxiety of the aged in contemplating the swift tide of change in the present age.

It is commonplace in the West to assume that the young must rebel, as their elders stand by, timidly protesting the brashness of youth, or patiently awaiting the coming of their maturity when youth itself will begin to show the wear and tear of years, and with responsibility, settle down into the grooves of tradition. Sophisticated societies have become fairly smug in facing this familiar cycle in the growth process. And with the aid of educators and psychologists, they have learned to take it in stride as one of the rhythms of human history, both within the individual and in group life.

The situation becomes somewhat less manageable, however, when, instead of being a rhythm of irregularity in an otherwise orderly life, or simply an interim of innovation in an overly complacent society, the revolt against historical sensibilities and values takes on widespread cultural proportions. The Modernist movement in Europe and the United States at the turn of the century and after was such a revolt. Modernism, though it is to be identified historically as the third cycle in the liberal movement of the modern period,[1] was a distinctive movement within Western culture beginning in the nineteenth century, following from accumulative advances in the sciences—particularly the formulation of the theory of evolution—and industrialization. It represented a more radical departure from the inherited sensibilities and values of Western history than either the Rationalism of the Enlightenment or the Romanticist era, and it opened the way for a new mythos in Western imagery as well as a possible new ethos of thought. An apt though extreme characterization of the modernist spirit as it appeared among European painters of that period has been given by the Indian art critic, Manchar Kaul, who, interestingly enough, finds this same spirit appearing in Indian art as represented by the "Experimentalists." Kaul writes,

[1] I have given a further elaboration of this thesis in my article on Theological Liberalism in the *Encyclopaedia Britannica*, 1965 edition.

Not only was the spiritual bond between God and man severed, but both got displaced from the high pedestal to which previous generations had raised them. Scientific knowledge and thought undermined religious belief in the hereafter, in God, and in the spiritual entity of man. True to the prevailing spirit of the times, the art of painting surmounting the inhibitions imposed by conventional modes as to themes, techniques, style and social obligations, turned amorphous in their bid to experiment and research in the region of the unknown. In the proud isolation of their fertile imagination the revolting artists spurned all constraint and compromise and cut asunder all mundane ties.[2]

I speak of this characterization as being apt, though extreme, because it designates precisely what modernism tended to become in its most secularized expressions; though it presents the modernist in too iconoclastic a role to be descriptive of the movement in religious and philosophical thought of the period. Here modernism was more restrained in its reactions, exhibiting a better sense of history and of developmental processes linking the present with its past. Nevertheless, the attitude that modernists assumed toward the past, as being a more elementary stage of present actualizations, giving it at best the value of a necessary antecedent, impelled them to move beyond all historical formulations and judgments as a matter of principle, on the assumption that growth and development implied, and therefore required, such an advance. This, then, was not a case of rebel individuals resisting or rejecting their elders, but an instance of the cultural mind at certain levels critically asserting its advance beyond traditional standards on evolutionary grounds.

As a cultural movement, however, Modernism must be considered a peripheral occurrence. That is, it erupted among those intellectualists, principally within the academic

[2] Manohar Kaul, *Modern Trends in Indian Painting*, New Delhi: Dhoomimal Ramchand, 1961, pp. 144-5.

community, who could participate in the critical ferment of ideas being evoked by the impact of the scientific understanding of man, his beliefs, and institutions, as evolutionary doctrines tended to reconceive them. It was essentially a revolution in the life of the mind, altering ideas, presuppositions, and points of view. It affected less radically the moral life of man and his sensibilities. Somehow the ethos of inherited proprieties and responsible living persisted among religious and philosophical modernists even as their theories of life and of man's destiny seemed disruptive and revolutionary in implication.

This last observation should be qualified somewhat, for in certain respects the modernists improved the moral tone of Western life. The modernist was deeply ethical. In fact, one could say that ethics was his religion. Whether Jew or Christian, Moslem or Humanist, the modernist of the West seized upon the moral imperatives of the inherited faiths as being their central core, and as being the one aspect of its history that could be deemed relevant, to the present world, if not normative in its religious judgments. Thus they rewrote doctrines and creeds, dispensed with ceremonial "trappings" as they called them, in order to accentuate the ethical thrust of these inherited faiths. They then set to work applying their critical powers of thought to this moral heritage and refining ethical judgments. In this sense the ethos of inherited historical values persisted with them, refined and reformulated to concur with present insight and judgment. For this reason I have often recoiled from speaking of this earlier modernist-liberal movement in Europe and America as secular in the usual Western sense of that term, i.e., as being devoid of religious restraint and directives. If it is secular, it is so in the current Neo-Hindu sense of "directing the spiritual vision of man to purposive action in present history." There is, in fact, a marked similarity between the modernist-liberal movement of the West and the Neo-Hindu movement in modern India.

We are witnessing today in modern America and Europe a far more pervasive and radical dissolution of historical sensibilities and values than occurred in the Modernist movement of a generation ago. These years since the close of the last World War, which, interestingly enough, coincide roughly with the era of India's independence, have brought about a mass relinquishment of historical guidelines, not only in science and philosophy, literature and the arts, but in public morals and in cultural attitudes generally. The iconoclasm involved here has assumed a variety of forms, ranging from a radical relinquishment of former proprieties in social practice and taste, along with the disavowal of restraints governing public and private morals, to an overt release of bitterness and hate in individuals and groups, and a readiness to resort to acts of violence as a direct and decisive way to attain the desired ends in a situation of conflict.

When one speaks of the breakdown in public morals, or of the disavowal of restraints in society, the word "Hollywood" generally comes to mind. This, apparently, for many areas of the world continues to be the conventional image of the modern Sodom and Gomorrah. Actually, if recent journalistic accounts are to be trusted, Italy, Greece, France, and Sweden appear to be far in advance of this Hollywood image, and England and Holland are well on the way to establishing their distinctive brands of moral deviation. These assessments by the press, we are told, are based on the rising wave of sexual license outside of marriage among European adults, the increase in illegitimate births among teen-agers and university young women, and the open declarations of independence from common public codes of morals among European intellectuals and other sophisticated members of society, particularly among political celebrities and actors. In saying that the reputation of Hollywood has been overshadowed by this European dissolution of morals, I do not mean to suggest that Americans are far behind in this new-found freedom. Evidence of a similar dissolution of these sensibilities is to be found in the frequent discussions of concern over campus morals and juvenile delinquency in the United States, and in the unabashed ventures in living as one likes with indifference to conventional codes, which finds justification in appealing to what is called "The American Sexual Revolution."

When a mood of revolt of such proportions breaks upon a culture, one is put to it to know how to account for it, or how to understand or assess it. So many forces and influences could be behind it. Along in the 1920's and 1930's it was common among social critics to assume that this modern assertion of sexual freedom could be expected in cultures plagued with the Puritan tradition. Breaking away from conventional standards of behavior in such instances, so the accounting ran, was simply a way of throwing off oppressive restraints which had made these natural human functions appear abnormal and perverse. Freudian psychology was the usual authority for this kind of analysis, and it also provided the leitmotif of modern novels and dramas concerned with exploring the mysteries of this new freedom. In the person of the analyst, Freudian psychology assumed the role of relieving the modern person from this burdensome superego which a Puritan tradition had laid upon him, and thus, presumably, released him to live out his life without the complications of moral compunctions. The outcome, however, was not always as rewarding as the Freudian had planned. But the interesting thing is that the countries in which revolt against traditional standards is now being most obviously flaunted can hardly be said to be of the Puritan tradition; though in each instance one sees in the background of the culture an assertive orthodoxy in religion which has achieved the status of a national or established church. Undoubtedly superegos can sprout from Prayer Books and Breviaries as well as from moral catechisms, though perhaps not as readily. In any case, it would be difficult to specify any one particular form of moral tabu that is being opposed in these present-day disavowals of morals. If the analysis applies at all, the reaction is against the notion of organized and established tabus as such, implying a custom morality, however sophisticated. When one probes this matter further, however, one finds that the current mood of revolt goes deeper than a reaction against a religious tradition or establishment. Basically, it turns out to be a rejection of all historically formulated absolutes, whether religious, philosophical, or political in nature.

Commentators upon this situation have been arguing for some time now that this dissolute attitude, which seems to be gaining momentum in Western society, is the aftermath of World War II. Society as a whole, they point out, becomes remarkably acceptive of irregular behavior under the stress and strain of war nerves; and whatever contributes to a release from tension can be rationalized or even justified. But this aftermath, if it is just that, has been stretching out over a long period of time. And many who are now being caught up in the ways of moral "freedom" were not even around to acquire war nerves two decades ago. Nevertheless, the cultural consequences of war cannot be wholly dismissed as giving background to what is presently occurring in society. What arose from the ashes of bombed cities, desolate landscapes, and concentration camps was but a specter of living death—people who had been deprived of all they possessed, including a purpose for living, if not their will to live. In place of ideals and human values, which stood

out as stars in the heavens at night to their romantic forebears, there appeared for these victims of the war experience the stark absurdity of this shattered human existence,
and the haunting realization that only death could bring re-
lief from it all. This note has been emphasized in the Existentialist literature of Western Europe, of which the work,
No Exit, by the French philosopher and dramatist, Jean
Paul Sartre, is pointedly expressive. But the most poignant
voice in this vein was that of the late Albert Camus, the
French novelist, who was killed, ironically, in a way that
documented his own philosophy, by a collision on a high-
way while driving at high speed.

This Existentialist literature is not simply a voice of
despair, speaking out of the disillusionment of a postwar
generation; it has a resolute theme as well, one that affirms
humanity and its realization of the authentic self. But it carries within its rationale a clear rejection of previous historical guides to such authenticity. As living men, during the
holocaust of war, were stripped of all that had given them
incentive for living, so in this bitter respite from war, cyni-
cally spoken of as the time of peace, they who survived the
holocaust were led to see that they had been stripped as well
of all the resources of Western history which had given
definition to such incentives. Existentialism is our most
poignant and articulate rejection of historical guides as such
in the West, and may give rise to a rejection of their coun-
seled restraints as well. Yet, curiously enough, it retains, in
some of its expressions, sensibilities historically identified
with the Judaic-Christian mythos, especially as these bear
upon human relations. With much else gone as a visible
support to human existence, the very fact of the encounter
between human beings, and the realities of spirit that can
arise out of such encounters in the concern of one person for
another, in human caring and companionship, not to speak

of affection and love, take on an importance that assumes priority over every other concern. A vivid depiction of this Existentialist theme appears in the writings of Simone de Beauvoir,[3] and it was implicit also in all of the late Albert Camus' writings.

Existentialism is thus a halfway house beyond the age rejected. It is more renascent than revolutionary, more a plaintive lament, giving rise out of a spiritual rebelliousness to a measured affirmation of life under the conditions now offered. Its response to the new age of nuclear power and the exploration of space appears to be one of indifference and skepticism, comparable to that of the modern Idealist's response to modern science a generation ago. It finds new bearing, not in any innovating facilities or achievements of man for extending the power structure of society, but in the human spirit itself. Man as man, Existentialism holds, is the only resource to which modern man can turn. In the affir-

[3] See Bernard Frechtman (trans.), *The Ethics of Ambiguity*, New York: Philosophical Library, 1948, esp. pp. 135ff. This theme is exemplified in various of her novels, based on the ambiguities of human relations in the last war as experienced in French communities, as in *Le Sang des Autres* (*The Blood of Others*), 1948, and *The Mandarins*, 1960. See also *The Prime of Life*, 1962.

The late Martin Buber, writing out of his Jewish heritage, lifted this theme of encounter between people to a significantly high level of analysis in his widely read classic, *I and Thou*, a book which has been singularly influential among contemporary theologians and philosophers of religion as well as psychologists. See also his *Between Man and Man*.

It appears to me to be a striking fact that this marked concern with sensitivity in human relations should occur simultaneously in this generation with exaggerated expressions of crudity and violence. Both the Existentialists in the West and the Experimentalists in Indian literature, as we shall see, address themselves to understanding people as human beings in their own right and destiny in opposition to using manipulative or tyrannical controls which deny this inherent freedom of the individual. This concern with sensitivity in relations stands in sharp contrast to the instances of egoism and arrogance which pervades much of our public life. This, I think, is a phenomenon to give us pause, if not some measure of hope, in that our sights concerning the realities of man in his spiritual dimension may be attuned to the problems of human nature that erupt in any given generation.

mation and nurture of man's authentic selfhood lies his only hope.

Not all that has emerged from the ashes of war and disillusionment, however, can be described as renascent and affirming. And this points to a more disheartening aspect of Western secularism. The lurking suspicion that only "nothingness" lies beyond the life of man has dissipated in some Westerners what little moral reserve or compunction may have imposed restraints upon their conduct, or given to their existence some substantive pattern of living. Under these circumstances, what Karl Jaspers has called the "life-order" shrinks to the proportions of sensual satisfactions, and to the routines of regret or delight which these demands can bring to the individual. Much of this indulgent activity is a kind of sedative to those absorbed in it. For their peace of mind requires insulation from thought, reflection, or even reverie. Many of the people who are caught up in this mode of existence are attractive individuals in themselves. They tend to be delivered of censorious attitudes. They are acceptive and responsive toward their companions. Their philosophy is to live and let live. And within the intensity of these relationships they derive intermittent moments of sensing that life is good. Thus an aura of general well-being, however deceptive, can pervade the associations of these individuals. Having accepted the limitations under which these years of life are offered, they are able to sustain an attitude of abandon which gives them a sense of freedom toward all inhibiting circumstances in life. It is this that makes them appear irresponsible, even dissolute, to those about them for whom a larger and more enduring life-order is regulative and alluring.

One can understand this secular stance, now appearing in increasing proportions among the new generation of European moderns and elsewhere in the West more readily if one is ready to see it as something more than an indulgent or brazen sexuality, or a defiant revolt against traditional mores. For many, at least, it is a respite from what living would otherwise be, given their vague sense of nothingness beyond these years.

To be sure, all rejection of restaints is not to be gathered under this understanding view. There is explicit delight in engaging in perversity for its own sake, which can only appear as gross evil to any sensitive and discerning mind. This problem has plagued and confounded theologians and moralists through the years. Dignifying such obvious perverseness with the caption of secularization is but a misuse of terms. Yet even here, we are being cautioned by social analysts and psychoanalysts to withhold judgment in specific cases until the life-history can be heard and examined.

We have been speaking of deviations from historical moral standards in our time which have followed from the loss of morale and from the breakdown of cultural syntheses in thought and practice which have hitherto given an accepted style to living. Much of this deviation is compensatory in character, seeking to salvage some degree of satisfaction out of immediate moments of living, where long-range purposes or commitments have become dissipated or disavowed. It is possible to speak of some of these adjustments as being pathological, though this conceals, or obscures, the vitally human issues that are involved here. Complacent and conformist thinking can thus dismiss these instances of deviation as being simply immoral or sick behavior, and thereby pass over too readily the critically human predicament that speaks out from these situations, involving not the few, but the many, and expressing not a bizarre and exceptional example of modern behavior, but one that is becoming all too common where dislocation and disillusionment with past values persist.

Certain contemporary theologians,[4] concerned to distinguish between these pathological instances of moral deviation and instances in which ethical issues underlying deviation are more sharply in focus, have set the problem in a different light. Under some circumstances, this view would hold, moral deviations may be seen as a release from erroneous or outmoded moral judgments stemming from a faulty theological interpretation of our human vitalities and of experiences following from the exercise of them. Thus, Paul Ramsey, Professor of Religion in Princeton University, has argued that to speak of sexual experience simply as sin is to profane the act unduly. In an article of striking candor, he writes, "An act of sexual intercourse is an act of love." He then adds:

It is also an act of procreation. Whether or not an existing relation between the man and the woman is actually nourished and strengthened by their sexual intercourse, the act itself is an act of love which had this power. Whether or not a child is engendered, the act is in itself procreative. This means that sexual intercourse tends, of its own nature, toward the expression and strengthening of love and toward the engendering of children. Let us call these two goods, or intrinsic ends, of sexual intercourse its relational or unitive and its procreative purpose. These are chief among the goods of marriage.[5]

This concern to take sex out of the category of the sordid and to lift up its beneficent, even its divinely ordained, as-

[4] See D. S. Bailey, *Sexual Relations in Christian* Thought, New York: Harper, 1959; Karl Barth, *Church Dogmatics*, Edinburgh: T. & T. Clark, 1960, Vol. III, Part 2, pp. 274ff.; Peter Bertocci, "Toward a Christian View of Sex Education," in *Sex and Religion Today*, Simon Doniger (ed.), New York: Scribner's, 1953, pp. 178-9; Harvey Cox, *The Secular City*, New York: Macmillan, 1965, Chapt. 9; Reinhold Niebuhr, "Christian Attitudes toward Sex and Family," *Christianity and Crisis*, XXIV (April 27, 1964), 73-5; Paul Ramsey, "A Christian Approach to the Question of Sexual Relations Outside of Marriage," *Journal of Religion*, XLV, 2 (April 1965), 100-118.
[5] Ramsey, op. cit. p. 100.

pect, is itself an expression of a new freedom in dealing with the historical sensibilities involved here. But it proceeds from a critically reasoned reassessment of those sensibilities, not a rejection of them. The intention here is not to deny or to condone the evil potential in sexual experience, and the perversions practiced; rather, it is to set them in a perspective which accentuates the depth of such evil since it profanes what is a valid human act.

In a similar way, Ramsey counters the common assumption that premarital sexual relations are categorically and in all instances wrong. The argument here turns on whether such a relation is "the expression and nurturing of a covenant love," and whether the covenant of marriage is to be identified with "the ceremony of marriage and the legalities of civil registration," or acknowledged in advance of these formalities as being the reality of a relationship which in fact they celebrate and seal. "The modern period with its standards of bourgeois respectability," says Ramsey, "has identified marriage with the ceremony and civil registration." "But such was never supposed to be the meaning of marriage before the modern period," he adds.

The older Christian tradition never had any difficulty in extending to what are nowadays called "premarital" relations what is nowadays called a compassionate judgment. In fact it gave no one but the parties themselves the competence to render any judgment at all upon such preceremonial sexual relations between engaged couples. In the "external forum" of neither the state nor the church had anyone the right to say they did wrong.

The very opposite was the case. The presumption was that they did the right thing. The presumption was that their betrothal consent to be married in the future was changed in the "internal forum" of their consciences into a present consent to marry before they engaged in sexual relations. The presumption was that they were fully, responsibly married without the ceremony and before their acts of sexual love, which were then an expression and the nurturing of the bond between them. This bond, their marriage, was present by their own making preceremonially.[6]

This theological reinterpretation of sexual experience, particularly as it is related to premarital experiences, offers sympathetic counsel and understanding to young people caught in the critical, and often unmanageable, circumstances of genuine love. Taken as a blanket endorsement of all premarital sexual experience, or as an easy rationale for what is plainly a dissipating adventure, it can be misleading and destructive. What is to be observed in these theological statements is that current practice is being reinterpreted, not simply on a basis of rejecting or dissolving historical sensibilities *in toto*, but by countering a recent set of tabus with what is regarded as a more venerable, and possibly a more authentic, historical precedent—a precedent that gives greater freedom to the exercises of the sexual experience in a context in which the realities of the experience of love and marriage are, presumably, more adequately understood and assessed. This shift in the Christian understanding of sex is viewed by its interpreters not so much as a secularization of life, implying the abandoning of historical sensibilities and values, as a reconception of the Christian view, based upon a selective appeal to these sensibilities. Those who assume a critical approach to the guidance of tradition and of historical values in the contemporary culture readily recognize that such guidelines are ambiguous until they have been selectively understood and interpreted. Many diverse views and judgments enter into any tradition. What functions within any culture as a continuing tradition is a distillation of past wisdom that seems pertinent and defensible within

[6] Ramsey, op cit. p. 112.

a given context of experience. Tradition works as a sustained intention within a culture to bring the seasoned judgments of its experience to bear upon its current history. But traditions become fragmented. In Western history this has been notoriously true, particularly within Christian experience. Clusters of nonconformist and separatist traditions exist side by side with, yet independent of, older historical strands of that tradition. What we are seeing today among Christian theologians, influenced by the new ecumenical spirit, is a repossession of the longer history of the Christian tradition, and a selective reinterpretation of its normative guidelines. This has the effect of setting this newly established legacy, distilled from the culture's longer history, over against more recent formulations of that heritage, such as the Puritan or the Liberal-Bourgeois conventions of morality.

But where a society is open to innovation and to the critical review of experience, the seasoned judgments that come into the current period as a legacy of the past are always subject to reconception, based both on the demands of new knowledge or new experience, and upon revisions in the understanding and assessment of the historical witness itself. Where there is this kind of critical and responsible attention to the claims of historical experience, and to sensibilities and values distilled from such experience, one cannot say that the social or moral deviations from historical guidelines within the culture imply a secularization of its life. This would be to make historical experience binding upon contemporary life in an absolute sense and to conceive of its judgments or sensibilities as being singular and unambiguous, which they certainly are not. These deviations, when guided by a critical reassessment of tradition in the light of issues raised by the current history, are to be regarded rather as being consonant with the sustained intention of tradition, and as functioning within its orbit of meaningful experience. It is in this sense that a liberalizing movement of life within any culture is to be differentiated from a secularizing force that works on indifferently or even hostilely toward historical sensibilities and values, seeking to be dissociated from rather than to continue within its orbit of meaningful experience.

Yet there may be circumstances within a culture's history that will impel the living generation to turn its back upon the past and, out of a concern to bring integrity and sanity into the contemporary experience, to reject it. Nowhere is this being more dramatically demonstrated than in the attitudes and outlook of modern German youth. For them, historical sensibilities, going back to their grandparents, represent the nightmare of Nazi perverseness and national hysteria. They are convinced that it was a fanatical nationalism that led to their degradation as a people. In their determination to escape the brooding sense of guilt under which they find their parents living, so as to be themselves on terms that are manageable and productive within the present situation, they are openly rejecting that past that centers in the nation, preferring to be known as Europeans, rather than as Germans.[7]

In a modified way, one finds African youth speaking in a similar vein. Here the breach between past and present has been widened by revolutionary political events that make the transmission of historical legacies to the present too difficult to manage. Thus, in effect, they are impelled to settle for what the present can provide, with little or no concern about any past heritage of sensibilities or values.

[7] Lloyd Shearer, "A Report from Germany Today," *Parade*, June 13, 1965.

These instances of dissolution are readily understandable. They do not represent weakness or failure in character or in the human psyche, but rather a renascence of human creativity and vigor that seeks authenticity in its own terms when shorn of all supporting resources. They represent, too, a native integrity in the human spirit which can rebel against corporate evil, however internal to one's history, in the interest of authenticity, instead of acquiescing to it or being victimized by it. What thus survives in character and in the quality of existence may turn out to be not as radical a mutation or dissolution as may first appear. For in such instances of human innovation, prompted by the desperate need to be self-fulfilling, what is asserted may not be simply a rebel reaction, but the salvaging of a selective strand of human dignity out of the debris of destruction that has been wrought within the culture. And in that sense, revolt becomes a prophetic ferment, cleansing the life stream of the haunting memories and emotions that would perpetuate what has been destructive. That there is loss of proportion in any such reaction goes without saying; but one can only say that in its selectivity it probably brings forth what can be assimilated to the present moment of decision and affirmation.

The urge to be oneself, to be free from encumbrances of a past heritage that abnormally constrains one, has played a role in most of the cultures of the West, even where there has been no occasion for traumatic reactions. In part, this represents a change in the style of living, motivated by demands of realistically accepting life as it actually is, and to put aside idealizations, pretensions, and expectations which tend to obscure or even to falsify the realities. This change in cultural sensibilities in the West became noticeable following the first World War; but it gathered momentum in the 1920's, and has progressed steadily ever since.[8] In this zeal to rid life of its sham and cant, we have succeeded in depriving it, too, of many of the civilities and courtesies that gave a measure of grace to living in former generations, and which assured it some sense of structure, consonant with a well-ordered manner of living. The sensibilities manifest in these responses of disciplined living, and the desire to be attentive to them, became suspect, and then expendable, as one by one the forms by which they were sustained fell into disuse. Initially, no doubt, the break in social decorum and other formalities in human relationships was intended to bring about a more genuine sense of community among people. It was directed toward extending the democratic way of life, and of bringing a greater degree of integrity into daily transactions as well as into public occasions celebrating and promoting that common life. Formal patterns of behavior were looked upon as being barriers to such genuine rapport, and were thus thrust aside. Informality became the order of the day.

This change in the outward style of living, relinquishing patterns of behavior by which restraint and discipline in human relations were nurtured, has had its counterpart in the inner transformation of the person. Personality studies have multiplied, addressing themselves, presumably, to this same task of establishing the person on a firm basis of reality, and of evoking in one the kinds of responses that could be justified rationally. The earliest influences in this direction also drew upon the Freudian thesis that the individual suffers from the domination of a "superego," and from unconscious drives which, on analysis, reveal stored up fears, resentments, and various interrelated anxieties. Thus, enabling

[8] For a graphic depiction of the style of living in late nineteenth-century America and the years of the twentieth century during its first decade, see Henry Seidel Canby, *The Age of Confidence*, New York: Farrar and Rinehart, 1934.

the person to "face reality" in this context, implied getting rid of those inhibitions or restraints by which the superego was able to dominate the self. The superego became a kind of modern mythical construct in sophisticated discourse for all idealizing agencies of the mind, which were to be dismissed as romantic reverie; as well as for religious and moral conventions, which, being judgmental in effect, were considered to be more serious obstacles to the person's freedom to act rationally. Furthermore, and this was considered more serious than their obstructive effect, religious and moral scruples, it was said, contributed to building up inner pressures in the person, giving rise to neurotic, or even psychotic, behavior. Accordingly, this demonry wrought by the pursuit of ideals and religious faith had to be exorcised. The fact that psychological and psychiatric studies have since modified this earlier Freudian thesis, and in some instances rejected it, has not removed the social effect of the Freudian myth centering about the superego; or the social consequences following from what was considered to be the solution to personality problems: namely, to give vent to feelings of anger or irritation, rather than to suppress them. There can be no doubt that some real gains in the integrity of human relationships and in the psychic health of individuals have followed from this release from dependence upon outward proprieties and from the tyranny of irrational pressures; but there have been unhappy if not disastrous consequences as well. One is the increase in unrestrained aggression and egoism in public transactions and places. No doubt much of the aggressive and egoistic behavior that is met with in public places comes about as a result of many people "doing what comes naturally," as the salty lyric goes; but it is clear also that substantial encouragement and justification has been given to relinquishing restraint and sensibility in modern society by these professional procedures, bent on improving the psychic health of individuals, without adequately taking into account the social consequences of such counsel and procedures.

Whatever the causes, we are being confronted in our time with an unprecedented display of self-indulgence, egoism, social crudity, and arrogance in day-to-day transactions. And the frequency and intensity with which this unrestrained arrogance and egoism assumes mass proportions, in the form of rioting and wanton acts of destruction, poses a major threat to the continuance of an orderly society, or even of orderly government, particularly within democratic cultures.

But the question arises, Are we not to distinguish between wanton aggressive acts, and outbursts of indignation or mass uprisings in protest against civil injustices, or against a nation's display of folly in the exercise of its foreign policy? This opens up another aspect of the problem of sensibility in the modern age. We have noted that the observance of sensibilities in social conduct has been questioned psychologically. Sensibilities have become suspect in our day on other grounds. Critical observers of the social scene have discovered how sensibilities can function as a smoke screen for shutting out ugly realities that plague society: practices of social injustice, racial discrimination, and poverty, not to speak of organized crime and corruption in the civil service. Individuals, sensitive to the ethical demands raised by these social problems, have felt the need of addressing themselves directly and vigorously to such issues, putting aside all counsel of restraint which may be offered by people of sensibility, who seek to avoid conflict and violence at any cost. This is by no means a simple matter to resolve. Conscientious and socially concerned people are to be found on both sides of the issue. Those who have become zealous in pursuing a course of social action in behalf of justice and integrity in public life have chosen to take part in picket lines and boycotts as ways of expressing protest against existing evils, and of participating in what is assumed to be a concrete step toward righting these conditions. And they have little or no patience with those who recoil from such overt acts on grounds of sensibility or propriety. On the other hand, those who turn away from such demonstrations, but who claim to be equally sensitive to the social issues involved will argue that nothing of consequence is achieved by these bizarre acts, except a hardening of factions that makes further understanding and negotiation between the contending groups less and less possible.

You in India have a vast amount of social experience and experimentation to contribute to the analysis of this issue, beginning with the earliest ventures in civil disobedience under Mahatma Gandhi and Jawaharlal Nehru. In fact, much of what is occurring in the United States at the present time in the way of protest marches and sit-down strikes in behalf of civil rights claims to have drawn inspiration from this historic Indian experiment in civil disobedience. Many, to be sure, are quick to point out, too, that the notable historic precedent lying back of the Indian experiment was the advocacy of civil disobedience by the American naturalist, Henry David Thoreau; and our historians and columnists are reminding us now that such acts of civil disobedience are in the best American tradition, dating back to the War of Independence between the American Colonies and Great Britain. The mere reciting of venerable names associated with such acts would seem to lift them to a new level of status. To be in the company of Gandhi and Nehru, or of Thoreau and the American Colonists, is not altogether discrediting. Yet acclaim by association is probably no more justified than guilt by association. In any case, to resolve the issue this way leaves many questions still unanswered.

The issue here has often been presented as one that comes down to the relative merits of revolutionary and evolutionary methods. One may say, it is not a matter of sensibilities at all; but a difference in perspective upon issues and problems within which sensibilities and judgments arise, and in terms of which solutions are sought. This issue between revolutionary and evolutionary procedures was very much to the fore in the heyday of the Indian experiment. There were Indians as well as Britishers then who were ready to argue that Indian Independence was on its way, and could have occurred, with or without Gandhi. Without him, some of your countrymen argued, the transition could have occurred with less brutality and bloodshed. Historical instances of colonies that achieved national independence within the British Commonwealth, such as Canada, Australia, and New Zealand, seemed to them to give precedent for arguing that independence through evolutionary transitions remained a possibility. Such a conjecture, however, can now have only the force of a supposition. History records that India's independence came about within a context of events in which the civil disobedience of Gandhi and his followers played a decisive role. And as such, it lends force to other contemporary revolutionary efforts, notably to the civil rights movement in the United States, and thus supports the claim that, under the pressure of an historical urgency within a cultural situation in which the appeal to sensibilities is employed to obstruct transitions toward human freedom within that society, a revolutionary break with historical sensibilities and values is made imperative.

However one may assess this claim, it serves to point up the fact that modern cultural experiences tend to support the argument that historical change cannot be attributed solely to evolutionary means, unless one can incorporate into its long-range occurrences the disruptive events which appear to break in upon and to break up the slower-paced ascendancy of events. Disruptive events of this kind, or crises, as they are sometimes called, generally reflect an issue of timing. The pressure of immediate demands becomes too acute to wait upon gradual changes of the historical process. Revolution then replaces evolution.

Now the tendency among historians and philosophers of history is to stress either the evolutionary or the revolutionary motif of historical change, and to make one or the other controlling in their interpretations of history. In a similar way, those who observe or participate in historical events as citizens tend to assume an evolutionary or a revolutionary stance in viewing or responding to present events. If nineteenth-century liberals were overconfident in their appeal to social evolution, present-day protagonists of social reform may be in danger of overvaluing revolutionary methods of social change. As spontaneous uprisings in protest against oppression, tyranny, or complacency, revolutions can be ethically justified in many historical situations. Under such circumstances, revolutionary acts express an understandable exhaustion of patience with oppressive, and possibly corrupt, measures of an existing government and an assertion of human dignity in protest against them. As a calculated method of reform, however, in advance of explicit provocation, and with a view simply to be assertive, or expressive of partisan demands, exploiting one's sense of power in any current situation, it can be dissipating and destructive of ethical sensibilities and judgment.

In this present stage of history, with revolutions enjoying unprecedented success the world over, and with a power struggle in progress between competing forms of world economy, one of which at least has openly embraced revolutionary methods of change as being essential to its success and survival,[9] it is clear that we are in for an excess of emphasis in this direction, however much we may try to restrain or discipline its use. This problem is too vast to be addressed in a cursory manner. My concern here is simply to call attention to the inherent risk of spiritual loss in any all-out capitulation to measures that flaunt all concern for the larger issue of sensibilities on the assumption that a man must exploit the balance of power that may come to him, or to his group, in any situation.

As we noted earlier, Western experience, particularly since the seventeenth century, has been oriented toward the future. Many cultural forces in the modern period have converged to engender in Western people a drive toward future objectives. History in this context has come to mean the on-going movement of life toward its future realization. So confirmed has this futuristic bias become that one social critic has observed, speaking of the American people, that, as a nation, we have become addicted to putting off decisions on the assumption that history would solve our problems. In this assumption we see the evolutionary view assuming the force of a national faith. Disdainful of the shallowness disclosed in this cultural outlook, one social critic has said, "History is no solution; history is our problem."[10]

It becomes clear, then, that the current disregard, or disavowal, of historical sensibilities and values is basically not out of accord with the prevailing winds of doctrine that have steered the course of Western experience. That these present acts of disavowal are more acute and revolutionary

[9] See John Kenneth Galbraith, "Poverty of Nations," *Atlantic Monthly*, 210:47-53, October 1962.
[10] Cf. Reinhold Niebuhr, *Faith and History*, New York: Scribner's, 1949.

goes without saying. And this, no doubt, is what makes them appear disruptive and even devastating in what they augur for the sense of meaning in experience. For it must be said that, despite its orientation toward the future, Western experience, in subscribing to the evolutionary outlook, has nevertheless retained a sense of continuity with past experience, even as it moved beyond it. Even though they sat lightly toward past valuations, or disavowed their authority, those who exemplified this Western experience generally assumed that they were reconceiving these historical intentions, rather than rejecting them outright.

What distinguishes the modern revolutionary state of mind in the West from this evolutionary outlook is its acute sense of breaking with the past, of disavowing all continuity with its intentions, assuming, in some instances, that any such continuity with the past could only mean a lingering sense of judgment upon present experience, and the defeat of the one desperate effort to wrest meaning from an otherwise meaningless existence. Here the whole of life's meaning appears to be telescoped into one urgent effort within contemporary experience, either to be lived out with intensity and with indifference to consequences, or to be pursued intensively as an act of decision. For those who have followed the latter course, decision in every act of living assumes the importance of the creative act, commonly attributed to the historical process, or to a cultural heritage. In this view, men are not shaped by circumstances or by a heritage of past valuations; they shape themselves by decisions of the moment that both initiate and commit one to a course of action.[11]

[11] The most explicit statement of this thesis has come from Jean-Paul Sartre. A brief but clarifying statement of it is given in his *Existentialism and Humanism*, London: Methuen, 1948. See also Simone de Beauvoir, *The Ethics of Ambiguity*, New York: Philosophical Library, 1948. A slightly different formulation of this thesis from within the Christian

In all of these evidences of the dissolution of historical sensibilities and values in the West, one sees varying degrees of secularization, ranging from a complete collapse of the spiritual sensitivity, implied in legacies from the past to a radical reconception of it. The problem of the West has been to assess these revolutionary currents of dissolution, and to distinguish between those secularizing currents that would deprive the culture of religious sensibilities and concern and those that remain deeply concerned for the spiritual life of man, though wholly dissociated from historical guidelines claiming to give authority and direction to man's religious sensitivity.

II

Flagrant disavowals of historical sensibilities and values are less in evidence in India than in the West, or, for that matter, than in other cultures of the East such as Japan and China. Despite the fact that the Indian people have been living through revolutionary events for more than half a century, something in their manner or style of living, be it forbearance, an instinctive adherence to past legacies, or sheer lethargy, has enabled them to keep the web of cultural relations relatively intact in the face of events that have been disruptive of relationships and loyalties. This turn of mind and spirit appeared to be present even in your most ardent revolutionary leaders such as Gandhi, and in liberalizing and liberating public figures like Rabindranath Tagore. Even Pandit Nehru at times disclosed that, despite his impatience with the social lethargy imposed by the historic religions of India, the sense of being committed to an historical heritage of the spirit deeply motivated him.[12] This turn of mind

---

perspective, as it functions in the secularized society of today, has been given by Harvey Cox, *The Secular City*, New York: Macmillan, 1965.
[12] See Jawaharlal Nehru, *The Discovery of India*, Calcutta: Signet Press,

is evident, too, in the attitudes of many of your public leaders today, particularly among your philosophers and other scholars and educators. This I report as a personal judgment on the basis of discussions I have been privileged to have with several philosophers and educators in your university communities.

As I indicated previously, they embrace the secular state, not as a departure from historical sensibilities and values, but as a present necessity which can be assimilated to historical procedures. This very fact I interpret to mean that concerned individuals in India are already at work, extending the historical vision of your culture to inform and direct its secularizing activities. This can be both an asset and a liability. It is an asset in that it keeps alive the historical vision of the culture in the context of its current affairs. It could be a liability, however, if, in their zeal to assimilate modern secularism to historical philosophical procedures, Indian philosophers became simply apologists for whatever takes place in modern India, so long as it squares ideologically with its heritage of ideas. From my acquaintance with some of your critical thinkers, I would not look for this kind of casuistry to occur, but it is always a temptation to the mind that deals with public affairs within an abstract context.

There is evidence, too, that modern Indian philosophers are addressing themselves critically and constructively to new issues being posed by the secular age—the concept of time, for example, in a world of change, or the metaphysics of relations. One article that came to my attention asked the question, "Is India's conception of time changing?" Another, "Must India's conception of human existence be looked at more concretely, instead of within the stereotypes

---

1946. An abridged version, edited by C. D. Narasimhaiah, was published under the title *India Rediscovered*, Madras: Oxford University Press, 1954.

of historical systems?" These, and other questions like them, alert us to the constructive ferment of thought that is at work among some of your thinkers who are sensitive to the bearing of the present turn of events upon your historical heritage and to the resources in that heritage for guiding present reflection.

The tendency is strong in your country, especially among your philosophers and religious thinkers, to assimilate change and innovation, even when borrowed from other cultures, to the historical vision and heritage of the past. Just as some of your statesmen and philosophers find ways of integrating the secular state, a necessary political expedient, to the socio-religious history of ancient India, so others among them are able to see in current philosophical movements like Existentialism, reassertions of historic Hindu ideas.[13] This would argue that there is a comfortable assurance among many of your philosophers and religious thinkers that your historical formulations and their valuations adequately express, or can contain, the sensibilities of thought conveyed in contemporary experience.

As one moves outside of academic and religious areas of Indian thought, however, one is alerted to tendencies that give indication of an incipient, if not an explicit, secularism that openly breaks with historical sensibilities and their formulations of value.

Not only has the scientific humanism and naturalism of the nineteenth century nurtured many of your intellectual leaders who have risen to influence in the modern period of India's political history, but present-day currents of thought, looking beyond the historical faiths, have found voice in some of your literary and philosophical writings, as well as in expressions of modern Indian art. I have caught

[13] See K. Guru Dutt, *Existentialism and Indian Thought*, New York: Philosophical Library, 1960.

glimpses of such evidence in various articles and books by your countrymen: one, an article on Hindi Literature in the *Orient Review* by S. H. Vatsyayan, and another, a book on *Contemporary Indian Literature*, published in New Delhi. What is disclosed in these two surveys is a striking similarity in tone and turn of mind between Indian writers known as Experimentalists (Prayogavada) and Western Existentialists. For example, "What is essentially new here," says Vatsyayan, "is the result of the new attitude toward man as a whole."

Having given up the search for, and the dependence on, trans-cendental sanctions, the writer has a completely altered picture of the predicament of man. Various consequences flow from this. The East-West schism becomes less important and rationalizations or other defense mechanisms seem unnecessary. The human sensi-bility is more important than an Eastern or the Indian sensibility; indeed, such adjectives begin to seem even absurd. On another level, the purpose of creation is no longer oneness with God, it is oneness with Man: the ultimate joy of creation; *ananda* is no longer twin brother to the joy of identification with the total sensibility of man. The writer is not pining in separation from the divine. He is much more concerned lest he lose touch with the feelings and emotions of man.[14]

In contrasting this new attitude with that of the past, Vatsyayan comments:

The Indian writer traditionally accepted his position in society and searched for the solitude of oneness with the divine: today the writer accepts solitude and seeks identification with the multiplicity of the All Man. Human experience, including human suffering and all human enterprise take on new dignity in consequence of this reorientation.[15]

[14] S. H. Vatsyayan, "Hindi Literature: Voyage of Rediscovery," *Orient Review*, III, 2 (March 1957), 24-5.
[15] Ibid. p. 25.

You who know Hindi literature well, and other indigenous expressions of the creative mind in India, may wish to take issue with this report. It serves, however, to point up a movement of mind among you which clearly resists, or, in any case, diverges from, the historic sensibilities and values which have informed and guided this culture. In this sense, one must say that this reorientation of the creative writer in India expresses a distinctly secular voice amidst all else which teems with a persisting devotion to tradition.

The Existentialist movement in Europe, as we noted earlier, voices something of this same nostalgia for relations with man as man among some of its writers, a probing of the elemental fact of our humanness; but these European writers have been more impressed with the denial of these basic human relationships in modern life, and with the absurdity that flows from this human plight in the midst of its technological trivia. Existentialism, in contrast to this Indian Experimentalism, seen from its barest intent, is the human outcry against what life has become and is; yet it represents, too, a total dissolution of confidence in or concern with the ideals, sensibilities, or presuppositions of past traditions that held out hope of a noble destiny of man, save as man himself affirms it and creates it. Its basic claim, following upon the Nietzschean lament, "God is dead!" is that Humanity is dying and will be forever dead except as man can assert his elemental humanness in a way that brings him authenticity and selfhood. Basically, you will see that there is something deeply spiritual in all these analyses of the human situation, however pathetic, something tenuously heroic, which can at times rise to an idealistic stand, but mostly it is an invitation to despair, which, ironically, counts on its naked stance to evoke a response of zest and determination. There can be no strength in man, it asserts, save as it comes from a bracketing out of all false supports, and a clear facing of the human reality in the starkness of its naked self-hood.

Bengali literature, in the main, appears to have continued the tradition of Tagore, which correlates nationalistic and universal motifs, as well as humanism and religious idealism. The secular voice is present here, but it does not seem to carry the note of rejection or relinquishment so dominant in Hindi writing, or in Urdu, or even in some of the recent Indian-Anglo writers. This could be because Tagore, in his own way, anticipated much of this reorientation of values that has assumed ascendancy in wider areas of Indian culture.

Similarly, in what I have read concerning recent Marathi literature, I do not detect a strong secularizing influence in the sense expressed by Hindi writers. There is innovation, especially in its poetry and short stories, and a breaking free of idealizations that simply romanticize existence. Reality in village existence is confronted rather realistically, and allowed to speak for itself out of the depictions set forth. But such resolution of life's problems as are attempted appear to draw upon traditional moral resources. In this respect, such secularization as is present here exemplifies that of which the Neo-Hindu speaks as "directing the spiritual vision of man to purposive action in history." It is pertinent to remark that what speaks forth here out of contemporary Marathi literature rests upon a secular urge that expressed itself as early as the seventeenth century, and which partook of influences of Western liberalism between 1885 and 1920, turning literature into a tool of revolt and reform.[16] Thus, as in Bengali literature, one may see that the secularizing influ-

---

[16] See M. V. Rajadhyaksha, "Marathi Literature," *Contemparary Indian Literature*, A Symposium, New Delhi: Sahitya Akademi, 1957, pp. 139-60.

ence was early at work in Marathi literature, anticipating in its way what has since become a more radical force of dissolution.

You will understand that I am speaking here more or less out of impressions gleaned from reports by your own countrymen. And certainly these impressions, as well as the selective reports on which they are based, may be open to question, though I find considerable concurrence of opinion among various commentators. A reading of Kaul's *Modern Trends in Indian Painting* reveals some of these same new turns in the sensibilities and imaginations of Indian artists.

It is important to note, however, that those who espouse this new liberating and secular spirit in Indian art and literature are unwilling to have their work interpreted as a rejection of values per se. Writing on Hindi literature in the volume on *Contemporary Indian Literature*, Vatsyayan observes that many superficial observers charge the new poetry with "a lack of faith or reverence, or value—or all three"; but this, he thinks, is to misconstrue their intention and to miss the reorientation of value which they intend. The new writers take these values seriously, he argues, but they face them as the realities of the human condition. There is, in fact, he continues, "a new and deepened reverence for values [in this literature] with a growing sense of their reality; a feeling of urgency in the task of reconstruction out of the shambles in which the writer found himself a few years ago. Never has the concern with values and the source of values been greater than today," he observes, "and of course no transcendental sanctions are sought and no values outside of man stipulated and human values are recognized as stemming from the common man not a conceptual Hero-man."[17]

[17] S. H. Vatsyayan, "Hindi Literature," *Contemporary Indian Literature*, A Symposium, New Delhi: Sahitya Akademi, 1957, p. 87.

This last sentence is the key statement, suggesting the nature of the reorientation of values that is at work in this secular vein.

Perhaps the most decisive and pervasive currents of dissolution at work in Indian society, moving it away from historical guidelines and sensibilities, are the demands and influences stemming from industrialization.[18] We discussed one aspect of this problem earlier. As a result of these demands and influences, changes are occurring in the structure of family life, as well as in the structure of society itself, that cannot help but alter the cultural ethos, particularly as it relates to the Hindu mode of living. For neither the filial pattern nor the caste system are able to remain intact with the modernization of the cities, the migration of factory workers, and the strain which these changes impose upon human relationships. The changes altering the caste struc-

---

[18] While evidence of social change in the major cities of India, resulting from industrialization, is irrefutable, it is important to recognize that the impact of these modern institutions and procedures of industry upon the social structure of India can easily be exaggerated when generalizations upon it are made. This warning has been given and impressively demonstrated by Professor Richard Lambert in an informative study of factories and factory workers in Poona, a city in the vicinity of Bombay. (See Richard D. Lambert, *Workers, Factories, and Social Change in India*, Princeton: Princeton University Press, 1963.) The thesis of this study questions the common assumption that the "introduction of the factory system has certain institutional imperatives . . . which are instrumental in moving a society from one end of the polarity to another, from a static, acquired-status-ridden, tradition-bound, primary-group-oriented, particularistic, fatalistic society into one that is rapidly changing." "The factory," says Lambert, "is a much more differentiated and gentle graft . . . its imperatives are not nearly so strong as might be imagined and they are not moving in so orderly a fashion toward the modernization end of the polarity." He concludes his study with the comment, "If the introduction of the factory is to be the sole or even the major catalyst in the modernization of Indian society in terms of the transformation from *Gemeinschaft* to *Gesellschaft*, the evidence of the present study indicates that modernization may be a long way off." Pp. 16-17, 224.

ture of society are indeed far-reaching with regard to historical sensibilities and values. For so much of the Hindu rationale bearing upon this historical legacy presupposes the caste structure. But the problem appears even more acute with regard to changes in the filial pattern of Hindu life; for historically, this has been the chief means of transmitting these sensibilities and values, and the heritage of faith underlying them, from one generation to another. With young people now marrying and establishing themselves as a family unit in cities, remote from the filial center, and independent of its daily routines, the break in this process of transmission is marked, as young Indian families that have moved to the cities will acknowledge. And the indirect effects of industrialization, and the new freedom it provides between the sexes, offer further possibilities of secularization insofar as they encourage or give rise to marriage between people of different faiths. The social scientists concerned with this phase of social change in modern India have applied the term, "the third culture," to this group, implying, no doubt, that they introduce a stratum of social change in contemporary Indian life distinct from both historical structures and contemporary forms of modernization within that historic ethos.

III

Summarizing our observations, then, concerning both East and West, this secular disdain or indifference toward historic restraints and sensibilities may not be ascribed simply to reactions of despair or disillusionment, whether pathological or not. It arises in part out of a serious and searching disenchantment with the notion that the past should direct human affairs, and possibly out of an attendant conviction that the present offers and demands a reformulation of directives. In that reformulation of the guidelines of man's destiny, genuine conflict or resistance to historic restraints and sensibilities may ensue.

Here some difficult problems emerge. One is the troublesome question, how does the past actually live on in the present—what is its meaning as a continuing dimension of the present? Another perplexing question is, How *should* it live on as a directive or guiding social force? How pertinent or binding are its values for the present day? Those questions are too large and demanding to be manageable at this time; but we can offer one comment on them which may illuminate some of the present-day efforts to come to terms with this kind of secularization in various cultures.

It has become commonplace today, speaking within the idiom of modern metaphysics, to say with Alfred North Whitehead that the past is available to us only as a dimension of the present. It pervades the present as a qualifying depth of meaning and valuation insofar as there are structures of experience in the preesnt to receive these meanings and valuations and to convey them. To be sure, the past survives in dormant form in mausoleums and museums, in artifacts and literary remains, in historic markings upon the visible and the invisible terrain, awaiting the discerning eye of the present or the creative hand that may render them available to those who can attend their meaning. It survives, too, in the habits and passions of men and women, in the images of the mind by which speech is formed, in legislative decisions that give bent to deliberations and their subsequent decisions, in the continuing fund of ideas and explications of reality that inform or challenge educational theories. The past survives in ourselves as physical embodiments of this life of the spirit, in the very tilt of the head, the look of the eye, or the body's posture, conveying the residue of anguish or joy that has been etched into our being by the passage of years. The past is everywhere present among us as a persisting sign and force of time that has been lived. But these are all conditional factors and influences, conveying their legacy as a burden with which to contend or as an opportunity to receive and to fulfill.

The past as communicable meaning, as a living voice in the deliberations of men, requires something more than duration—something more than simply being there as an enigmatic command or censorship of the present. These meanings and valuations must be conveyed within the idiom of the present. The past must, in effect, die unto itself and be resurrected and reclaimed in the garb of present forms and symbols. This is never to do full justice to the glory of the past valuations; for only what can be received within the structures of experience among living men can be renascent, dynamic, creative within the present. And this may be meager, indeed. But meager as it is, it will be genuine in its appropriation when taken on these terms.

What may occur in such appropriations of past meanings may be so marginal as to appear to the ardent traditionalist as a sheer travesty upon the past. Insofar as these past valuations must be conveyed in forms so obviously modern, and possibly barbaric, they must appear as nothing short of a secularizing of the tradition. And, in fact, they are precisely that, if to secularize a reality is to lift what has been deemed sacred out of its hallowed setting and thrust into the vital operations of the living present. But secularization then may mean disinterment of a sacred symbol or image, thereby releasing its potential power into society as a social energy of immediate magnitude.

I should make one final comment on this form of secularization in modern cultures, which consciously disavows many of the historical restraints and sensibilities. To one looking on from a perspective of history, wherein, among cultures of the past, a high degree of qualitative attainment was possible, these present-day upheavals in one society after another will be judged iconoclastic, ruthlessly destroying the structures of life that have sustained its qualitative living. Quality, as it connotes discriminating judgments of intricate and subtle effects, giving depth and nuance to objects and their relationships, precision to definition and form, or propriety to expression—quality in this sense is a hard-earned achievement within any culture. Its responses come about through patient, probing association with things and relationships by which these artifacts and experiences of life are contemplated and enjoyed. Such qualitative attainment requires a degree of leisure and detachment from urgent demands. The hurried and impatient look will not be open to perceive it or to contemplate it. And thus it is possible that the concern with quality as a contemplative act will become a prerogative of those who, because of circumstances of birth or favor, are removed from the intensities of labor and decision in a society. Class structures have no doubt arisen among all peoples in some form as a consequence of noting or arranging for these distinctions among men. And it is possible, therefore, that quality, as it is known and acknowledged under such conditions, tends to be a sensibility applicable to the stratifications of these human associations.

The breakup of class structures in modern societies, releasing those who were bound by tradition and legislation to explicit levels of servitude, and thereby enabling them to participate in the full range of human activities and opportunities of the culture, immediately overwhelms all standards by which quality of attainment has been discerned. The sovereign hold of higher standards thus crumbles as the levels of society dominated by, but not informed by, such standards gain ascendancy. As a result, qualities of experience less carefully calculated or contemplated, but available and appropriate to the more arduous life of these lower strata, likewise assume ascendancy; and by the very mass effect of their presence and demand they displace the art forms of leisure and detachment. One may not say, therefore, that the revolutions of our time do not mean a tragic loss to cultures at the qualitative level of its experience, wherever they are occurring. Sensibilities of perception, delicacies in skill, performance, and appreciation; discrimination in the subtleties of thought, ritual, and religious doctrine—all these are deemed expendable in a time of cultural upheaval, when the world is bent on the distribution of basic freedoms.

One may understand, therefore, why the traditionalist, for whom these expressions of excellence are of paramount importance and have even spiritual connotation, protests so vigorously against this dissolution of historic sensibilities and standards. It is, in his view, a profanation against both man and God.

Yet, to the defiant ones, who see in their iconoclastic efforts the spiritual assertion of the human spirit in the name of bread and liberty, and in the name of extending human dignity and freedom to all human beings, "profanation" is but an ugly word. It can have no meaning in the world in which they move; for as Mahatma Gandhi is reported to have said on one occasion, "To the millions who have to go without two meals a day the only acceptable form in which God dare appear is food."[19] What is there to say in response to such human candor?

What Rabindranath Tagore sought to do at Santiniketan may be one answer: he undertook, on the one hand, to sustain the nurture of the traditional arts of India and thus to

[19] Quoted in C. A. Coulson, *Science, Technology and the Christian*, New York: Abingdon, 1960, p. 77.

uphold the qualitative outreach of its culture; and, on the other hand, to pursue village reclamation in a nearby center, looking to the needs of the people. Where both efforts are possible, holding the two emphases together and letting the one inform the other is certainly to be desired. But in deference to the actualities in most situations, one must acknowledge the realism of Gandhi's remark. One acts out of the demands of the historical situation. One is called, as it were, to give heed to what is laid upon one by the needs of the hour.

Is it possible, however, to be relevant and responsible to immediate demands without sacrificing historical vision? Is it possible to sustain sufficient historical judgment, even within the intensity of present zeal and zest for decision on urgent issues, to provide for qualitative concerns that transcend these issues? The style of a culture will determine the answer to these questions. If it is in the culture's history to be responsive to imaginative and reflective qualities of human experience, however remote from the urgent demands of public life, these qualities will be nurtured and sustained by someone, if only on a marginal basis, until they can assume more direct relevance to the business at hand. If, on the other hand, the stratifications of society are such that these qualities can be identified wholly with a leisure class, and thus made expendable when that kind of aristocratic leisure is no longer tenable under the pressure of urgent responsibilities, the concern with qualitative attainment in the culture will be relegated to the discard.

This is the true meaning of barbarism in any society, when the new life of a people, based upon elemental demands, must relinquish past attainments in depth and value, or voluntarily disavow them, thus sacrificing its qualitative outreach. Vision and proportion are thus abandoned in the interest of focusing all energy for immediate ends. The result can only be a relapse into immature sensibilities, wherein vigor and decisiveness are esteemed more highly than patience and reflectiveness. Where this happens, the assertive forces of society gain ascendancy as its deliberative, appreciative powers recede. This is a clear indication of spiritual recession.

The retention of historical restraint and sensibility in the face of change and advancing technical means is thus a mark of spiritual superiority in any culture. This need not be the same thing as a persisting traditional bent of mind in a society. Traditionalism is an aging process that resists growth and change. Retaining historical vision and sensibilities in the act of coming to terms with change, and of assimilating its invigorating energy is something else again. It is the simultaneous act of challenging the past to assume its present opportunity for survival, and of summoning the present to be worthy of the legacy of lived experience which history transmits to it.

The Significance of Religious Sensibility and Wonder in Any Culture

One conclusion that is being drawn from the present turn of events in modern cultures, where secularization has been a dissipating force, is that all historic religions have been rendered obsolete. I shall undertake to deal with that judgment later. A second, more serious observation which is being made today is that religious sensibilities and the sense of wonder are no longer relevant to a technological civilization. The posture of man generally presupposed in such sensibilities and response, it is argued, no longer obtains now that man has aggressively addressed himself to exploring every conceivable aspect of reality and is so successfully opening up hitherto concealed areas to human enterprise, turning its energies and resources to the use and betterment of mankind. Ethical values, appropriate to the conduct of affairs in the human community, it is conceded, can be seen to be imperative; but sensibilities or responses expressive of anything more than this would seem to be incongruous with what a technological civilization implies.

This judgment is by no means a recent one. It is at least as old as the scientific attitude stemming from Francis

Bacon. And it has motivated much of educational theory as well as social and philosophical reflection since Positivism became a generally accepted world-view among educators. What is recent about it is the widespread assent to it among moderns, young and old, following from the magnitude of scientific achievement, and thus the vividness of its contribution to every sphere of life. It is this that has enlarged the public image of science as a benefactor of mankind, and, conceivably, as the source of its salvation.

No discerning person will brush aside this judgment lightly. I must say, in all honesty, that it is a judgment with which I have lived during all of my mature years as a student of religious history and philosophy. I have confronted it, pondered and probed its meaning for modern man and his cultures, at times feeling the force of its claim, but more continuously sensing the shallowness of its understanding of man in the full dimensions of his being.

To put it bluntly, this judgment that religious sensibilities and wonder are no longer relevant, now that we have entered upon a technological civilization, overlooks the basic fact that, despite all the accomplishments of men in the exploration and use of his natural environment, the posture of man with reference to the ultimate dimensions of his existence, as marked, for example, by birth and death, has not changed. The context of human existence still presents to each of us a sense of something given, to which we are related in elemental ways. However far we develop and use our human powers, we do not slough off this elemental condition of being creatures of a Creative Process that is not made by us, not really influenced or altered by us in anything that our sciences or philosophies undertake. It is given as a primordial fact of our existence. We can obscure this sense of creatureliness, block it from view, proceed with the business at hand without thought of it, and, in our sophistication, we can disavow it. But this changes nothing except our attitudes and states of mind. The realities of existence presented by this elemental fact of creaturehood persist as ineradicable circumstances of this living context.

Let me pause at this point to make a distinction which I think may be helpful to our discussion. In speaking of the significance of religious sensibility to any culture I am using the term "religious sensibility" in a rather restrictive and specific sense. If one assumes that by religious sensibilities one means simply the characteristic feelings or responses of those who are sensible to what concerns religions, our confusion will be confounded. If, however, one takes religious sensibility to imply responsiveness to what ultimately claims man, supports and judges his ways in the light of this primal context, one will be looking beyond religions as such, and beyond all human responses evidencing such behavior to the sovereign good that is the source of all religions and that stands in judgment of their human ways.

When one distinguishes between religious sensibilities and the religions, one is implying, of course, that not everyone who manifests religious sensibilities is a participant in some religion. And, on the other hand, one may imply also that not everyone who does participate in the overt forms of religion is expressive of religious sensibilities in their most discerning sense, or in a sense that renders such a response relevant to the cultural life of a people. I am talking, you see, about a kind of response that is appropriate to every human being, regardless of his faith or culture, by reason of his participation in a primal context that is given in existence.

But now I move to a second observation. Not only is there a primal context in which our lives are cast, there is a specific context, a particular dimension or level at which our creaturely existence occurs—the human structure, it is sometimes called, as differentiated from all other natural structures. This fact, that we are in a sequence of evolving structures, and that we constitute one characteristic structure of life at a specific level of differentiation, implies both the range of our possibilities and the limitation under which we exist.

Now let us note parenthetically that, while the human structure has a distinct set of facilities consonant with its level of emergence which are peculiarly its own, it retains certain other features which mark its solidarity with antecedent forms of life: a bone structure, internal organs, a blood stream and a vascular system, etc. This body-life of man is a miniature repository of much else that antedates the animal structures. The sea water that flows in our veins, carrying salts and minerals, giving substance and seasoning to our internal workings, recalls our identity with the prehistoric deposits of rock and soil, and our continuing solidarity with this wondrous environing nature.

Yet, mind you, the human structure is dynamic in nature. It is not just a static repository of substances derived from antecedent forms; nor is it an arrested level of existence in every respect. It is volatile and eruptive with psychic disturbances, some of which arise out of its own sensitivities as a psycho-physical organism, but not all. Some of these disturbances give outlet to anxieties, wonderings, and outreachings that are expressive of what William James once called our tropism toward the More of existence.

Religions have been quick to mythologize this More of existence that seems to supervene our characteristic structure; thus we have fully elaborated accounts of its nature. Unfortunately, these accounts are so varied and contradictory that, to discerning and critical persons, they tend not to encourage confidence in the fact of this more ultimate ground of sensitivity. The truth is, we have only marginal apprehensions of it, such apprehensions as our limited structure of life affords. Yet these apprehensions are sufficiently acute to alert us to the tenuous intimations of a level of sensitivity reaching beyond our attained level of existence.

Thus, we may say, man as an organism has a natural history; but as an emergent spirit he appears to be within an orbit of existence that points him beyond his characteristic, structural attainments, to a "thither-side" of his presently evolved structure. Accordingly one may speak of man as having his representative structure as human being, i.e., the facilities of personal existence that are native to his level of existence, and this outreach toward something More that evokes responses in him.

With this general view of our existence in mind, we may be able to come to a sharper understanding of what is involved in religious sensibility and wonder. It is, first of all, a capacity in man to be aware of himself as being a creature at one level of existence, and thus mindful of certain structural limits. To put it baldly, certain explicit senses (five in number) give him access to a certain range of occurrences. These can be magnified and subtly differentiated in fantastic ways, as we have seen in these latter days of radio and television. How much farther parapsychology will extend this sensory range of the human being we have yet to learn. Yet the basic sensory limitation remains.

More positively, I have intended to suggest that this religious sensibility and wonder appears as a capacity in man to be tenuously and intermittently aware of yearnings or intimations transcending his structural existence. In my *Realities of Faith* I undertook to establish a working concept of the reality of spirit as man's relational ground with whatever constitutes this More of existence. In that discussion I quoted John Donne's familiar line, "No man is an island," and then commented that, On the contrary, every man *is* an island; but islands are not what they appear to be, isolated bodies of land. When one probes the shoreline one finds that, at a deeper level, every island is related to a land base that extends to a mainland and that unites each island with other islands in the sea. Now I cannot build a philosophy on a figure of speech, but this figure of the island and its relationships may help to make vivid a philosophical claim that proceeds quite naturally from the conception of man's emergent structure. And I use it only for that purpose. I subscribe, as you can see, to a metaphysics of internal relations which, in turn, has affinities with the modern vision of relativity physics. This will come out more clearly later.

A sense of wonder, therefore, is not just a vacuous outreach toward a great empty Nothingness, but an expectant and somewhat apprehensive openness to what is envisaged in this relational ground. All firm concepts of such a ground are hazardous, and probably misleading; but I am insisting that we have intimations of its meaning in concrete relations which are sufficiently discernible to give us a sense of what such an ultimacy can mean. One such intimation is the notion of context, which I mentioned earlier—the context of each individual existence marked by birth and death. There is an entrance and an exit defining the visible bounds of concrete existence, which can suggest to the critical mind either Nothingness as a context, or a Creative Passage in which life is given and in turn received. By this point I mean to suggest only that there is a dimension of the Given in our existence, an aspect of it which is not in our hands to command, and which has not been shaped by human hands.

Furthermore, I would hold that our relational ground is intermittently discerned in the relationships that hold us in existence. These are numerous, but the ones most revealing are those in which a good that is not of our own making comes into our existence as a grace that is given. In moments of dependence, when the grace of another's concern for our well-being or the grace of an affectionate relationship reaches us, we are made aware of such a good not of our own making. To be able to receive such grace that is given in existence gives some inkling of what transpires at more primal levels of our existence which we cannot observe or consciously attend.

Now as I said earlier, the fact of this wider dimension of the human spirit can be brushed aside in our sophistication as modern people. And it is quite understandable that many of our contemporaries should choose to focus upon the clearly marked traits or features of our presently emerged structure, taking these characteristic human capacities as being defining and normative of the human person and his order of life. One can establish an impressive order of life on this basis. Most of our workaday world proceeds on this basis. Certainly our political and economic spheres of society conduct affairs within this clearly defined orbit of existence. Much of educational theory and practice proceeds within this delimited dimension of our humanity, and the tendency to follow this course is accentuated wherever education is directed toward competent and successful living in a technological age. Even certain modern forms of religion may be found which settle for this representative human dimension of life, and thus they seek to formulate regulative and directive measures for assuring a responsible and morally rewarding human existence on this basis. Religiously speaking, they are saying that ethics is enough.

It may not be improper to speak of these orders of life, which consciously confine their commitments to the characteristic and representative structure of man, as forms of voluntary isolationism; that is, as ways of looking at man and his community in isolation from all other structures of existence, and thus to ascribe autonomy and ultimacy to man simply as man.

Perhaps you can see, then, from what I have said thus far, how the problem of secularization takes on added dimensions in this context. You will recall that, in speaking of the modern state, we differentiated between a secular state that conceived of its secularization as being constitutive, and one that viewed secularization as instrumental. The one became closed and inhospitable to everything save what served its immediate ends; the other sought to pursue its urgent and immediate ends within an open society, responsive to criticisms and judgments which might arise within its society, and able to negotiate when dealing with the differences that inevitably emerge. Speaking now in the terms which we used in commenting on the modern secular state, this human isolation, when it is asserted in all spheres of the culture, limiting the orders of life to this representative structure of man, imposes upon the culture a secularization that presumes to be *constitutive*. It tends to render the total cultural outlook within its purview hostile to whatever would transcend the human community. Now it can be argued, much as we argued in discussing the modern secular state, that the political and economic life of man must proceed as secular activities, uncomplicated by the nuances of religious sensibilities and wonder. Ethical values, looking to the exercise of just and orderly processes and to the integrity of human relationships, will certainly be imperative; but more than this need not be required—except one thing: a policy of openness and toleration toward those enterprises of man that do pursue the meaning of man within a larger orbit of existence.

In all other enterprises, however, the arts, education, philosophical, religious, and even scientific inquiry, such isolationism, implying a constitutive secularization of modern culture, will act as an unnecessary and detrimental closure upon the culture. Their function, in each case, does not demand that they be secular, either in a constitutive or in an instrumental sense in the way that other processes of society might or do. And their role as cultural disciplines, nurturing and expressing the human spirit, and extending the range of its possibilities under the limitations of its existence, would be immeasurably enhanced were they to remain open toward this total reality with a sense of wonder. Needless to say, the cultures in which the creative, aesthetic, and reflective disciplines could be attuned to the full dimension of the human spirit, and free within a secular state to exercise these functions, would likewise be enhanced, if not actually blessed.

But it is probably oversanguine to expect that these critical disciplines will readily respond to such an appeal. It may not, however, be either utopian or uncritical to insist that, when these disciplines, in their zeal to be heard or to be decisive, make their secular disavowal of religious sensibilities assume the finality of a dogmatic claim, they relinquish the right to be known as a critical discipline, concerned with critical inquiry, and become instead another form of apologetics for a constituent secularism.

Now what has been distinctive about the historic religions has been their openness to a dimension of reality beyond the human sphere of existence. We need not elaborate upon the various ways of acknowledging or responding to this vision of reality. Much of what is conveyed through formal and doctrinal statements or ceremonial practices rests, as we have said, upon mythological constructions which must be taken to be the poetic and dramatic extension of primal insights or intuitions. The philosopher of religion and historian of religion will be attentive to the rich tapestry of mythological creations as creative expressions of the human spirit, and as possible indices to what is basic in the human response to the ultimate dimension of existence. While he will not take the full doctrinal and ceremonial history of any religion as being the inevitable and final expression of this primal religious sensibility, or of the profound sense of wonder that inheres in or underlies its religious forms or exercises, he will value them, along with the institutions that currently convey them, as being the present carrier of that primal response within that particular culture, and as being its persisting, motivating mythos. In saying this, you will see that I am distinguishing between myth and mythology. The latter is an explicit ideological projection of this sensitive awareness into an imaginative and dramatically creative lore, either as a direct expression of the creative impulse or as a didactic means of explicating and propagating the witness of faith arising from these primal sensibilities. Myth, I would hold, is not to be identified wholly with mythologies. Rather, it is the persisting sensibility and sense of wonder, abstractly referred to by Rudolf Otto as "creature-feeling," functioning within any culture or community of people as a dimension of depth in their existence. It is, in short, the historical and deeply organic expression of what I earlier termed "the tenuous intimations in the human structure of a level of sensitivity, seemingly reaching beyond its attained level of existence." The persistence of this sensitive awareness of what is at work in the human structure, motivating and impelling it beyond its own ends and capacities, is what keeps the individual organism and the communal life alive to the full dimension of its existence and meaning.

Thus while mythologies are expendable, myth, as a persisting expression of this primal response of sensitivity and wonder, is not. For our human rendering of what is involved or meant by the primal creaturely response is constantly subject to modification and correction, or reinterpretation, as cultural history proceeds and as cultural forms and the idioms of thought and speech change; but the sensibility in man, giving current history to the primal response as a sense of wonder and anticipation of the fullness and depth of his creaturely existence, is an elemental capacity in man that persists wherever man is left free to be open to the total range of his organic existence.

We noted a moment earlier that cultural man, through studied and disciplined effort, can shunt off these tenuous intimations of sensibility and wonder beyond his own structure; and through neglect or habitual indifference to them, can establish a life-order that is neither motivated nor consciously qualified by this sensitive range of spirit open to the human structure. The common life, thus shorn of this appeal to sensitivity and wonder beyond its own norms, or of sensibilities that can render man responsive to it, will suffer a deficiency of spirit that will become delimiting, progressively enclosing its norms and purposes within the demands of the cultural experience. Man's experience then becomes the sole measure of his ways. Men so committed to becoming characteristically human may thus be made statically human: that is, a community closed within those established concepts of moral good that the cultural experience can achieve and sustain. What is lost from this social vision is the sense of judgment or challenge that can come from a transcendent measure, or from a sense of limitation in the human structure which will forever keep one open to and inquiring about the validity of human forms and formulations.

In one respect, both the humanistic decision to adhere to the characteristically human dimension of existence and the procedure of religions to mythologize the transcendent outreach and live rigidly within these doctrinal definitions tend to come to the same thing. Each of them, in its own way, encloses man within the forms and fantasies of the historical culture. In both instances the religious sensibility and sense of wonder, expressive of the primal response, tends to be lost sight of, and, as a consequence, the resource of judgment or corrective in its transcendent reach beyond all creatural experience is made nonexistent. Without such a resource, self-criticism and openness to judgment of the ways of one's religion or one's culture tend to atrophy or to disappear altogether. This has been the story of our historical religions as well as of humanistic ventures presuming to counter their claims.

The will to look beyond cultural norms, and to establish a world outlook in faith or in politics has, on the other hand, generally followed the course of emptying thought and policies of all cultural coloration, including its religious biases; and this has meant not only secularizing the international ideal, but also abstracting it from all concrete involvement in the sphere of cultural differences. Internationalism, or what is at times called *universalism*, thus assumes a strangely artificial character as a vision of man deprived of all concrete references, and dissociated from cultural involvement or commitment.

The look beyond cultural norms need not imply this disavowal of cultural involvement and commitment; any more than being attentive to dimensions beyond the human structure need imply a disavowal of our humanity. It need recognize only that cultural assessments and interpretations of experience are limited, and thus fallible, just as the human structure, as a distinctive level of emergence, is limited, and thus to a degree fallible, liable to the errors of its limitations. Yet, within these limitations and fallibility, both cultural experience and the human structure are capable of creativities in thought and act which are expressive of its indigenous character, and as such, are not only valued outlets of self-expression, but valuable contributions per se to the total drama of existence. These human creativities within any culture are to be cherished, nurtured, and sustained, but they are not to be absolutized any more than the human structure itself or the mythological renderings of the primal outreaches among religions are to be absolutized. Holding all of these creativities and formulations answerable to a higher level of sensitivity, or at least open to judgment, even as we cherish and sustain them, can enable us to look beyond these structures, even as we participate in them, and promote their indigenous goods amidst the differences of other cultures, other religions, other creatural forms.

Furthermore, the very spirit of mind expressed in holding one's own creativities and formulations subject to the judgment of a more ultimate level of sensitivity can enable one to be critical, yet measured in one's response to the historical religions that arise within one's own culture, even as one acknowledges and cherishes the truths they affirm, even as one participates in a religion as one's own resource and witness of faith. To have people in any religion who can exercise this kind of critical acumen, even in the interpretation of doctrine and moral judgments, is an asset to religions as well as to cultures.

In what we have said thus far, we have sought to identify the scope and quality of the religious sensibility and wonder we envisage and the contribution it can make to the vision of a people, giving openness and outlook to the culture as well as a critical sense in attending to its own creativities and judgments.

Where there is outreach beyond the human structure, the religious sensibility and sense of wonder arising from it can contribute to modern cultures in other ways. It can actually bring into the common life resources of a kind that appear as a surplus of goodness which comes into existence out of the relationships that hold men in existence. The Christian religion has spoken of this surplus of spirit as *grace*. The Bhakti devotion in India, going back to the Hindu philosopher, Ramanaja, presents a similar characterization of it. This resource of grace is an empowerment of life and purpose that is not of one's own calculating effortfulness, not at one's bidding or command, but comes as a gift, as one says, where there is the capacity to receive what is given. The capacity to receive what is given implies an orientation of life, a stance, if you will, that is itself expressive of religious sensibility and wonder. It implies, first of all, that something can only be *given to me*, for it is not mine to command. This goes back to a very old premise: "The earth is the Lord's, and the fullness thereof." That is one expression of it. You may recall many others. This premise stands as a restraint upon the energetic drive of modern men and civilizations, bent on getting what they want, and upon the so-called enterprising spirit of modern man and civilizations stemming from the time of Francis Bacon and the Industrial Era of the West, when initiative and enterprise in compelling nature and the processes of men's labor to yield up their goods was first vigorously asserted as a principle around which to organize scientific and political activity. Cultures in the West have become addicted to this stance, and have fortified it in some sections of the community with moral directives, sanctified by religious doctrine.

What has given cultures in the East, prior to this recent period, a sense of spiritual superiority over the West stems in part from their instinctive response of aversion to this spirit of unrestrained enterprise. Yet, at the same time, they have recognized their own physical inferiority to the driving power of the West; and, for a time, they suffered under the imperialistic extension of Western control. But the ironical fact is, so it would appear at least, that, having been released from the imperialistic control of Western powers, Eastern cultures, one by one, seem to be relinquishing the premise that once gave them a sense of spiritual authority, and instead they are adopting the spirit of aggressive enterprise to remove or to correct their social ills.

On the surface this turn of events would appear to be a clear instance of secularizing the cultures of the East, not only imbuing them with a spirit that is alien to their history, but causing them to forsake historical guidelines that are indigenous to their religious traditions. I dare say that some of the resistance that one detects among reactionary groups in Eastern cultures to this so-called Westernization of its life stems from this kind of analysis of the modern situation.

Yet it requires but a moment's pause to realize that to dismiss as secularization those programs of action and reform that are so desperately needed to bring hungry men and women the bread and rice they need to sustain life is simply to enhance the word secularization. We are confronted here with a paradox. The paradox may be more apparent than real, but it nevertheless evokes profound confusion in present-day thinking on the crisis in modern cultures. The paradox seems to be that the cultures of the West, with their spirit of initiative and enterprise, stand under the judgment of the age-old religious premise, common to East and West, but more consistently sustained among Eastern cultures; yet to assure its people life in a time of unprecedented need, the East must avail itself of this spirit of enterprise, and thereby incur the risk of spiritual regression.

As in all paradoxes, this one conceals discrepancies of logic upon which the terms of the contrast are built; only in this instance, they are not discrepancies in the logic of thought, but in the logic of history, as it has been lived both in the West and in the East. If the spirit of human initiative and enterprise in the West has tended to obscure the primal religious premise that the earth is the Lord's, and that to this Ultimate Ground we are beholden for resources of grace, the response of the East to this primal premise has wreaked its own form of cultural havoc. In the words of one of the most revered statesman of the modern age, the late Jawaharlal Nehru, who in his lifetime was bent on revising the course of action in India, this response of Eastern cultures has been to encourage a spirit of fatalism, the cultural consequences of which have been lethargy and indolence in coping with the practical problems of human livelihood. When applied to specific situations, these observations may appear very wide of the facts. As generalizations upon the prevailing moods of West and East, however, they speak a truth that is sobering beyond anything we can presently imagine.

It would be audacious of me to presume to find a way through this modern dilemma, the issues of which have challenged the best thinking of statesmen and seers of both East and West. Yet I have been impelled to apply every energy of thought I can muster to contribute whatever earnest reflection can bring to bear upon it, hopefully to break through the impasse in some slight respect. To that end, I invite you to consider one insight that appears to me to be relevant to the discussion. It has to do with the way we conceive of man, or more particularly, the way we conceive of man's relation to whatever is considered divine. The basic premise which I offer, as a ground for reordering our thinking about man, and for revising his response to the primal religious premise, is this: The conception of man as being related to a higher order of sensitivity does not disavow the propriety of man's individual initiative and creativity. It does, however, imply a condition of dissonance in the relationship between man and the transcendent Good which at one and the same time affirms man's freedom to be creative and assertive, as well as his need to be responsive to the judgment of the level of sensitivity that transcends and cradles his human structure. Put in traditional terms, man's commitment to God does not nullify the command to exercise man's human powers of creativity. The dissonance arises from the interplay of authentic centers of selfhood, in which freedom of self-expression is acknowledged and the freedom to receive another's expression is affirmed.

Neither the typical Western mind nor the representative Eastern expression of religious and cultural thinking, in my judgment, has adequately acknowledged this complexity in their concepts of the divine-human relationships. Both, in a way, have assumed that divine transcendence implied domination of the human spirit, either on the ground that the divine, being other than man, stood in a relation of judgment toward man, or on the ground that man, being less than God, was therefore subservient to Him. Consonant with this premise, the will to freedom in the West has generally implied man's alienation from the divine, and in proud but sensitive Westerners, for whom the authentic existence of selfhood has meant life itself, such a state of mind has led either to a forthright disavowal of the divine dimension or to a form of pragmatic humanism which, for all practical circumstances, dismissed this dimension from consideration in human affairs. In the East, subservience to what was deemed divine superiority has left the will of man docile and accepting of conditions imposed. Insofar as the East has partaken of the spirit of Western humanism, and has sought to elevate the human spirit, it has felt duty-bound to equate its human idealism with ultimate goodness itself, and thus has tended to merge divinity and humanity. Interestingly enough, except for the most recent efforts in Neo-Hindu-ism, this high valuation of man has not turned Indian thought to the task of improving the plight of man in his present existence; rather it has led it to explore the intricacies of the human mind and spirit on the assumption that it was thereby exploring divine dimensions of existence. Spiritu-ality in the East, particularly in Indian thought, has thereby come to imply every kind of esoteric manifestation or exer-cise which could lay claim to being another facet or nuance of personal existence.

Those, in turn, who have been awakened to the need of more direct dealings with the practical concerns of human living have been led to disavow all such preoccupations with mystery and mysticism, as did Pandit Nehru, and to address themselves to these social tasks on a scientific basis in de-fiance of any appeal to spirituality. In this, modern Indian secularists have joined hands with the Western scientific humanists to rid the world of all obstacles to a scientific un-derstanding of human problems, out of a concern to attack them directly on this basis. It is no accident, I think, that the writings of Bertrand Russell have been so widely read in India. He speaks for a formidable group of Indian minds who have dispensed with spirituality as Indian thought has conveyed it.

We see, then, that both East and West have tended to view this relationship between the human and the divine as being one, either of subservience or resistance, conformity and identification, or rebellion and alienation. Conformity and identification have led to the concern to re-enact the divine life in man, to the neglect of man's human initiative in expressing his distinctive structure of existence. Rebellion and alienation, on the other hand, have led to a determina-tion to assert or to pursue the human dimension of man with indifference toward divinity, or any transcendent dimension. This pattern of subservience or rebellion, determinism or freedom, in religious thinking about God and man has precluded any notion of a negotiable relationship existing between the structure of man and the transcendent. Yet it is precisely this kind of relationship that most accurately defines the interplay of divine and human structures. God, as a goodness not our own, has an integrity of structure that is what it is, a level of sensitivity and grace that stands unshaken or unmoved from divine purposes by the foibles and follies of man. Yet one can say He is moved by what we are and do in the sense of being responsive to us in His acts of judgment and grace. Man as a creature of God nevertheless has an integrity of structure that is what it is, a level of sensitivity functioning within the limits of its emergence, yet with an authenticity appropriate to its being. Man, too, is relational, yet solitary and individual. This is the complexity of his being. One can say he is made for God, for other men, and for himself. This is the formula that best expresses the interplay of the relational and individual aspects of his existence. As a conception of man, it expresses the dissonance that inheres in his existence as a given fact. He is possessed with a freedom to be himself, and, as a creature of God with a divine intent, he is obligated to pursue this freedom to fulfill that intent. Yet he has access to a freedom to be more than himself, free to be in relation to other men and creatures, and to be in relation to God. The true state of our humanity is defined by the demands with which these dissonant relationships confront our existence. And our negotiation of them is what ultimately characterizes our nature and destiny. The British-American philosopher, Alfred North Whitehead, was pointing to this truth of existence when he wrote in *Religion in the Making*, "the topic of religion is individual in community." This is a resolution of the issue which does not destroy the dissonance of relationships.

When that dissonance gives way, either to rebellion or to acquiescence, both freedom and responsibility are impaired in man; and the stature of man as a free, yet related being, deteriorates.

I would hold, then, that the source of much of our difficulty in retaining religious sensibilities and a sense of wonder in the modern era, or of relating them to the concerns of a scientific and technological age, roots in the fact that religious thinking has been dominated by a pattern or mode of thought which inevitably causes all such sensibility and wonder to issue in a piety of subservience. The humanist tradition in every age has been a proper protest against this kind of docility that denegrades the human spirit and the structure of its existence. But the folly of humanistic thinking has lain in the tendency of its protesting to move invariably toward a truncated, ethical view of existence which has disavowed the response of religious sensibility and wonder in man.

A proper relationship would seem to be one of genuine dissonance, rather than one of subservience in which one seeks to come to terms with the ultimate measure of life in the context of pursuing with seriousness and appreciation the known values in our human creations. In the Jewish and Christian Scriptures there is a story of the patriarch Jacob, wrestling with the angel, which I would suggest is an apt parable of the relationship between the human and the divine. And its meaning would imply a vigorous assertion of the human equation, even in confronting the measure of this ultimate good not our own. I would put it this way: In any encounter between the human and the divine, it takes a bit of doing on the part of God to get a good man down. Dissonance in this context is expressive of a serious and genuine encounter between concerned and qualitative levels of existence.

Yet, we are to do all this, not in lieu of our critical inquiry, but in the context of it; not in lieu of pursuing the completion of our human creations, but in the context of it.

Eventually this would bring us around to saying that, in acknowledging the transcendent aspects of our being as a structure of sensitivity in which our lives are cast, we do not deny or disavow the freedom of man to employ initiative and enterprise in attacking problems of well-being. Spirituality is not the denial of our materiality, not the denial of our body-life or of our humanity, but the summoning of it to be itself and more.

In this brief résumé of a working conception of man, I have meant to give the rationale for asserting that, in acknowledging the transcendent aspect of our being as a structure of sensitivity in which our lives are cast, we are not necessarily denying or disavowing the freedom of man to employ initiative and enterprise in attacking problems of well-being. On the contrary, we are suggesting that this effortful program of reform and renewal can be enhanced by religious sensibilities which alert man to resources of the spirit that inhere in relationships, and that can bring to bear upon these effortful labors, energies of grace "which can do for man what he cannot do for himself."

I come, then, to some judgments about the significance of sensibility and wonder in any culture. Religious sensibility, as we have been employing it, has to do with the response of wonder and sensitivity to what inheres in the human structure as in intimation of A-More-Than-Human-Reality, to which the human structure is related as creature to ground, and toward which it has instinctive outreaches. Sense of wonder is its elemental expression, issuing simultaneously, as the anthropologist, R. R. Marett, has observed in a response of apprehension and "vital joy."[1] Its mature

[1] R. R. Marett, *Faith, Hope, and Charity*, London: Macmillan, 1932.

and seasoned expression will be a steady openness of mind and spirit toward possibilities of goodness and meaning, transcending man's own measure of good. Sophisticated levels of existence can find common ground with what is less sophisticated in proportion to the individual's capacity to exercise this maturity of judgment that partakes of the elemental outreach. To the degree that the sophisticated person cannot do this, he dissociates his mode of discourse from the more common levels of humanity. And to the degree that one cancels out, from one's intellectual and cultural concerns, all semblances of sensibility or response which would convey a sense of wonder consonant with creatural innocence in the presence of life's mysteries and the exigencies of existence issuing in both good and evil, one forfeits a significant quality of one's humanity. The Christian scripture quotes Jesus as saying, "Except ye become as a little child, ye cannot enter the Kingdom of Heaven." This, I think, could be claimed as a true anthropological statement. Put in more explicit terms, Except one can retain something of the childlike wonder and innocence of elemental people in the presence of life's ultimate mystery, one is shut off from the depths of one's own being, and of life's meaning. For the claiming of these depths waits not on our own initiative in inquiry so much as upon our capacity to receive, in wonder and sensitivity of feeling, what is being conveyed to us in such moments of awareness.

Secondly, the presence of such sensibilities in men has a leveling effect, in the good sense of that phrase. That is, it creates a ground common to all wherein the primordial equality of our humanity can be envisioned, and where acknowledgment of limitations appropriate to the human structure can be made sobering and edifying. Man needs the elation of sensing the innate possibilities of his human creativity, but he needs equally as much the sobering and restraining effects of confronting his creatureliness. Whether this takes the form simply of seeing oneself as an individual in the context of the Species, as Feuerbach was insistent upon doing,[2] or of confronting the edge of one's being in ways that open up a wider horizon of transcendence, the reorientation of selfhood that can come with recalling this primordial dimension of existence can be both heightening and restraining in its effects upon the human psyche.

The common bond of creaturehood is at least preparatory to a sense of solidarity in relationship, either as human beings cast in a common lot and confronting common possibilities and perplexities or as beings in relation to a common source of human good, from "whence cometh their help."

It is true that, in morally awakened religions, the formulations of what God expects of man, as directives for human living, tend to lessen acceptance of the human condition, and thus tend to abound in moral censorship rather than in social sympathy or human kindness. Yet, when the crises of life come, or when human need or suffering becomes acute, the resources of sympathy consonant with religious sensibility are evident, and are generally expressed with generosity and a wholehearted sense of solidarity.

The absence of this resource from any culture becomes a major human catastrophe, as in Nazi Germany, or in instances of war or in mass uprisings when men encounter one another, not as fellow human beings, but as objects of hate, or simply as impersonal symbols of the enemy that is to be destroyed. Yet the absence of this resource can be felt in societies in times of peace through the impersonalization of institutional life and the mechanization of the processes of society in which human persons tend to lose their identity as persons, and the humane response is displaced with auto-

[2] Ludwig Feuerbach, *The Essence of Christianity* (1841). Paperback edition in English, New York: Harper & Row, 1957.

matic mechanical action. The magnitude of this mechanization in present-day technological and industrialized societies accentuates the possibility of dissipating this resource of human sympathy, and of thereby imperiling its humanity to a critical degree.

Thirdly, it may be said that such sensibilities in any culture provide a resources beyond the egoistic drives in a society, and thus contribute a restraint upon them. A moment earlier we spoke of the limitations of the human spirit that can arise from its total absorption in the human structure, with no reference in values beyond the norms and measures of its own formulations. This limitation of the human spirit stares out from the corporate transactions of society wherein motives of self-interest or gain, on the individual or group basis, tend to prevail. Where effort has been made to regulate or to elevate the tone of these transactions, the procedure has been to extend the concept of self-interest to embrace common interests, as in co-operative associations, or even in the United Nations. On the surface this reconception of the motive of self-interest would seem to be only an enlargement of the basis of interest, thereby bringing the self into accord with other selves. Self-interest, so it would seem, is thus made convivial or social without lessening the self-centeredness of the motive. In a sense this is true, but it is also true that this very act of relating one self to another, and of taking account of a horizon of interest, with its responsibilities that extends beyond the immediacies of one structure of existence, is of a piece with the movement of spirit in man that can reach beyond the human structure itself. It is but a step beyond the co-operative envisagement of common interests and goals to what Buber has called the I–Thou encounter, wherein spirit arises in man at a more sensitive level than in these utilitarian acts calculated to bring about a larger social good. Yet it is a step not easily taken. For this requires a contemplation of the *other* in and for itself, which implies a radical subsiding of egoistic drives in man. This relinquishment requires a degree of abandon or of trust in the bond of relationships that is not readily available to men steeled for action and accomplishment.

As one pursues this notion of relationship among individual selves, especially in a context in which individuality has assumed a high degree of freedom and self-consciousness, one will be led to see that one important path leading into the life of the spirit lies along this way: that is, that spirit as a good not our own, or as a resource of grace, is in relationships, not in any kind of relationship nor in every relationship. For relationships can turn in on themselves and become simply the human ego writ large, as in nationalism, or in tribes and clans. But wherever the fact of man's relatedness can summon them to acknowledge a good not their own, or the good of another, which simultaneously stands as good in its own right to be nurtured and cherished or as a resource of grace for other men when the occasion demands —wherever this can occur, the cultures of men can be called blessed. And in this kind of fabric of human relationships, the culture of the human spirit is significantly assured.

World Religions in an Age of Science

I have lived long enough to have participated in two periods of modern history in which the crisis of faith erupted as a consequence of the impact of the sciences upon religion. One was in the 1920's, when the controversy over evolution broke out afresh in midwest America. Evolution had been a familiar notion in Western thinking since the middle of the nineteenth century. Most critical thinkers in Europe and the United States thought that the issue had been thoroughly laid to rest. Thus they were shocked to hear that controversy over the issue had erupted again. But there it was. People of "the Bible Belt," as it was called in mid-America, had put everything aside to thresh it out again in a spectacular trial in Tennessee in which the venerable political orator, William Jennings Bryan, and the noted criminal lawyer, Clarence Darrow, were locked in deadly battle. The University of Chicago was near enough to this celebrated occurrence to be drawn into it, and to feel the repercussion of its arguments as they were reported by eye-witnesses, or by the daily press. We lived through that era and bore the scars of its battle during subsequent years, persuaded that the issue between science and religion had been finally laid to rest.

But of course it had not. The second crisis of faith came in the 1940's and after, following the release of atomic energy amidst the holocaust of war. This, too, was a delayed outburst, for much that was implied in the launching of this new age of power had been known among scientists as well as philosophers and theologians since the end of the nineteenth century, when the new vision of science first broke upon the scientific community, following from experimentations in radiation and X-ray. What was distinctive about the atom bomb, apart from its destructiveness, was the fact that its effects were instantaneously known to millions of people around the world. With one demonic blast, it made this new vision of science a public event. The millions were now aware of its presence, where heretofore only a small company of critical thinkers had been aware of it at all.

The release of atomic energy in itself was not the telling event, so far as the issue between religion and science was concerned, although the way it was used and the circumstances under which it occurred intruded issues of humanity which may not be dispelled in our lifetime. But even this was not what precipitated the second crisis of faith. Rather, it was what this new resource of power was to make possible in subsequent years of experimentation and adventure. For from the falling of bombs, we were to be catapulted to the launching of space ships and rockets, and to flights into outer space. Suddenly the expanding universe was to become illimitable in scope, and the world of Reality, once fairly well mapped, both by religionists and scientists, had become a No Man's Land, too big to envision or to possess.

The image of the expanding universe, now made vivid by actual flights into outer space, had a devastating effect upon the image of life conveyed through the historic religions, or even through the philosophies of various historical periods. In fact, what became evident as one listened to questions that were being asked or pondered, was that a depressing scent of obsolescence had fallen upon all historical legacies, particularly upon the historical religions. For the many religions of the world, so it appeared to many who were reacting under this state of shock, were but little clusters of ceremonial piety which had arisen in various cultures around the earth, along the river Nile, the Tigris-Euphrates, the Jordan, and the holy Ganges, as well as along or beyond the Danube. What a pathetically provincial spectacle these now presented, in contrast to the shining new horizon of outer space!

This kind of reaction was occurring, not among the sophisticates and intellectualists of the West, but among ordinary congregations of church people, skeptically listening to their preachers who were awkwardly trying to be both relevant and traditional, and among school children and college students, avidly taking full citizenship in the new age of science that was now so vividly upon them.

There were, of course, ready responses to these reactions, not only among religionists refusing to be intimidated by them, but by civic minded scientists, eager to demonstrate that not all was lost to the religious man, however alien the new world of science had come to appear. In this context, the cry for an ethical idealism, informed by the sciences, seemed a ready-made answer to all such queries, arising out of this pervading mood of disillusionment in the West. One of the most persistent spokesmen in this vein has been Julian Huxley, the British botanist and publicist, who for more than thirty years has been advocating scientific humanism with the zeal of an evangelist. His book, *Religion Without Revelation*, first published in 1930, has been reissued in paperback and is being read with renewed interest by many of the present generation. Speaking at a Convocation of Scientists at a Scientific Congress held at the University of Chicago a few years ago, Huxley reiterated his theme of scientific humanism with the fervor of proclaiming a new gospel for the atomic age. Moving into the atomic age, he argued, is as drastic and revolutionary a step in the ascent of humanity as was the transition that brought animal life out of the sea and established their habitat on land. The new age, he said, demanded a new religion, consonant with the vision and evolutionary understanding of man and his world. But the new religion he offered was the old one he had been propagating for these many decades. Then in a gesture of clearing the decks for a fresh start in being religious, he prophetically declared that the historical religions had reached the end of their evolutionary cycle. But, he added, we need not trouble ourselves about them, for they will die of their own accord, and one by one will disappear from the face of the earth.

More recently this note of finality for the religions has been heard from within the churches themselves. Among the younger clergy and theologians of several Protestant communions, it has become commonplace to assert that, in the West, we have entered upon a Post-Christian era. This is the voice of secularization within the churches, acknowledging, or, more accurately, confessing the plight of obsolescence in Christianity, and implying as well that such obsolescence applies to all historic religions, and to the ceremonial forms they employ. Two books in this vein have been particularly widely read and discussed: one, *Honest to God*, by Bishop John A. T. Robinson, formerly of Cambridge University, and a more recent book, *The Secular Meaning of the Gospel*, by the young American theologian,

Paul Van Buren.[1] The thesis common to these books is that

[1] Since returning from India, a book published during my absence dealing with this issue has come to my attention: *The Secular City*, by Harvey Cox (New York: Macmillan, 1965). This work, in my judgment, is a fruitful and provocative analysis of the issues bearing on secularization within religion and culture. Professor Cox distinguishes between secularization and secularism, pointing out that the former can have the effect of freeing religion and society from oppressive customs and traditions, while the latter, secularism, introduces into a situation of social change a new dogmatism centering in an ideology, "a new closed worldview which functions very much like a new religion." What is arresting about Professor Cox's work is the stance he assumes in confronting the new secular age. His emphasis is not so much on relinquishing historical notions and sensibilities consonant with Christian faith as seizing the present secularized occasions of history for initiating new ways in which to express and to effect the religious commitment. He conveys the same sense of abandon with regard to traditional religious forms and customs, and a breaking free of the inherited presuppositions and frames of meaning that is common to other writers on this theme. Yet he appears to have cut himself loose from the overweening concern about the meaninglessness of modern life, which has haunted so much of modern thinking and writing. Instead, he is intent upon discovering or experiencing meaningfulness in addressing himself to immediate occasions that claim him in responsible action. In so doing, he is able to draw upon a vast amount of biblical precedent and pragmatic understanding of meaning in encouraging the churches to take up their task in the secularized societies of urban communities.

Within a different context of problems, my colleague, Gibson Winters has addressed himself similarly to the possibilities being offered to churches in urban communities confronted with secularization. See his *The New Creation as Metropolis*, New York: Macmillan, 1963, and his *The Suburban Captivity of the Churches*, New York: Macmillan, 1962.

The work of Thomas J. Altizer should be mentioned also in this connection. Though in a different vein, and drawing upon resources gleaned from philosophy and the history of religions, Altizer comes to a similar affirmative stance in what he calls *a radical theology* addressed to exploring the eschatalogical occasions in the present period of history. The essence of what is relinquished of traditional lore and presuppositions is gathered up in the Nietzschean phrase, "God is dead." The confession of this negation, says Altizer, enables the modern man to take hold of present moments of existence with a fresh sense of their reality and opportunity as being demands upon him in his stark, human condition. Negation in this dialectical form of thinking, he argues, does not in itself imply a negative attitude toward religious commitment, but a clarifying and cleansing way of pointing existence away from illusory supports toward what is believed to be the only creative and fruitful way of affirming existence in its present moment. See "Nirvana and Kingdom of God," *Journal of Religion*, XLIII (April 1963), 105-17. This all established forms of carrying on the Christian witness through conventional ecclesiastical means are bankrupt. They have no currency acceptable to the modern age. Society has become secular, and understands only terms and acts that speak out of the workaday situations of the modern world. We must sit lightly toward all creeds, abandon our doctrinal and ritualistic niceties, and find our place at the side of our secular brother, to be there as one man ministering to another man in need of our humanity.

Both of these forthright efforts to secularize faith and to dissociate it from its historical context mean to be solutions of the task of religion in the face of modern secularization, and to be formulations of a religious response to this age of science. As I address myself to the general theme, *World Religions In an Age of Science*, I mean to speak also to these specific programs for clarifying the problem that is raised here.

At the outset, I must say that I welcome this forthright note of secularization in the churches. Anything that can rout the scent of sanctimonious religiosity in the churches can only be considered a cleaning force, a fresh wind blowing. It is not their secularization that I mean to challenge, but the presuppositions that prompt it, and thus the dubious consequences that may follow from it.[2]

Briefly, let me say, with all the authority I can muster as a philosopher and historian of religious thought, that the historic religions will not die, Julian Huxley to the contrary notwithstanding. They may degenerate, reform, and then

---

article also appeared in *New Theology No. 1*, Martin E. Marty and Dean G. Peerman (eds.), New York: Macmillan, 1964. See also Altizer's *Mircea Eliade and the Dialectic of the Sacred*, Philadelphia: Westminster Press, 1963.

[2] I have commented at greater length on each of these proposals in two articles: "A Voice of Candor," *Religion in Life*, XXXIII (1964), 19-27; and "Alternatives to Absolutes," *Religion in Life*, XXXIV (1965), 343-51.

renew themselves like the phoenix, but the ability of religions to accommodate themselves to environment and to participate in the changing cycles of evolution is disgustingly good. In this statement, I do not mean to laud or criticize the religions. I state it simply as a fact with which to conjure.

Nor do I see any enduring solution of the problem that is being created by this crisis of faith, in the atomic age, along the lines of a freewheeling secularization in the churches, although this movement has much to commend it. For the basic problem with which people of religions as well as those of the culture generally face in this new age of science has to do with a reorientation of the religions, both with regard to one another and in relation to the disciplines of the culture in which they exist. I shall take the second problem first, and then comment on the relation of the religions to one another.

Religions, whether they venture upon internal programs of secularization within themselves or not, confront the unyielding fact that, increasingly, they exist in and participate in secular societies. They not only have to do with secular governments, they confront a climate of opinion and judgment which tends to be answerable more to the findings of the sciences than to the teachings of religion or the reflections of philosophers. Science, in fact, has assumed an ascendancy in our time that is unprecedented in the history of civilization. This was inevitable, once the freedom of man came to be associated with a concern for the physical well-being of every man. For the sciences provided the special competence necessary to deal with freedom in this context, and the very magnitude of the task envisaged in fulfilling this dream to improve the physical well-being of every man, and to encourage every man to be free to demand it, put the sciences in business in a way that no cultural discipline has been socially applied. As modern cultures set themselves seriously to the task of meeting vast human needs, the demand for more and more disciplined understanding of the sciences and technology throughout the world sharply increased, and it continues to increase with a rising momentum.

The fact that the same new resources of power that made possible unprecedented advances in technology and industrial development also made possible the spectacular achievements in space exploration has given to scientific inquiry and experimentation a public prestige and influence which it has not known since modern science first emerged. Thus human need and a zest for exploring new frontiers that have been opened up to our generation combine to accentuate the status of the sciences in modern culture.

I have already commented upon the secularizing influences following from science and technology as they begin to shape more and more of the culture's life. There is another side of the story as well. The sciences bring to a culture a certain stature and integrity of effort which can be sobering and stimulating to any people. Amos Wilder, the American New Testament scholar, has observed that the sciences have attained a stature in pursuing their inquiries which no other cultural discipline of our time has achieved, or has been able to emulate. With this judgment I would agree. But I would add also that certain scientists of stature have attained something which previous generations of scientists sorely lacked, namely, a maturity of mind with regard to the claims concerning the ultimate cosmic implications of their inquiry. At best, these scientists of stature are saying, science, with all its precision and careful calculations in coming to its formulations, must put up with having to settle for occasional successes amidst numerous failures. Many formulas fail; others succeed. The successes are often fantastic and overwhelming, both in what they disclose and in their impact upon those who witness their feat. And by the very novelty and, in a way, the uncertainty of their outcome, these successful occurrences are accompanied by emotions of surprise and elation among scientists themselves. What this argues, then, borrowing Professor Ramsey's words, is that in the sciences we have "disclosure models" rather than "picture models," models that occasionally, or with some frequency, dispel the mystery of these processes through their disclosures. Scientists who are attuned to ultimate questions of a philosophical or religious nature readily agree with this view of their labors. This way of reconceiving scientific inquiry, in fact, was first enunciated by some of them. To be sure, even as the scientist assumes this tentative stance with regard to the ultimate meaning of his work, he will urge, as did Albert Einstein and Max Planck, that, despite this large element of chance in scientific inquiry, the scientist, in order to pursue his inquiries, must presuppose as a vision of faith that an orderliness in the universe exists. But the image of orderliness as a vision of faith is something quite different from a scientific dogma presuming to be a scientific description of orderliness, based on the observation of facts.

To the scientist who exemplifies this maturity of judgment in the philosophical and religious use of scientific inquiry, science is an ally of all who probe the meaning of our existence with sensibility and wonder. And he is the critic of all who would make absolute claims to a knowledge of ultimate truth about it, whether they be philosophers, theologians, religionists, or scientists.

What science is adamant about is that knowledge is relevant to a perspective, and this, too, it would claim, is as true of religious and philosophical knowledge as it is of scientific knowledge.

Now as a philosopher or religionist, one can be soberly informed by this judgment without being slavishly acquiescent to what the sciences say. As a participant in the cultural disciplines, however, one will feel the force of this scientific judgment about the nature of thought and the limitations of human experience. It is not, then, that the philosophers or religionists simply submit to the dictates of the sciences, but that philosophers, religionists, and scientists find themselves living and thinking in the same world of discourse and they accept the same limitations upon human understanding and the pronouncements that follow from them.

Both scientist and philosopher, along with the religious thinker, may acknowledge various dimensions of experience, conveying different kinds of qualities of meaning. Thus neither the scientist nor the philosopher need be confined to the level of inquiry pursued by the sciences, though in every instance what is sought at other levels will always be in a creative tension with what is disclosed through scientific inquiry. This is simply to say that to be a modern mind implies participation in all of the forms of inquiry available to present experience, to the degree that one is able to do so.

We come, then, to a crucial point in our presentation, bearing upon this theme of religious sensibility in a scientific age. I mean to argue that scientists, for all their magical and astounding performance in the use of their methods, have become impressively modest with regard to ultimate claims about man and his world. By their recognition of the limits of their procedure, they have removed the onus of dogmatism that attended so much of scientific naturalism or scientific humanism in years past.

But I would carry this observation a bit further. The principle of limitation which we discussed earlier, and which any careful study of the development of natural structures will be led to lay upon man's understanding, is one that is applicable not only to the sciences, but to every form of human inquiry and response, including that of the religions. One need not commit the fallacy of reducing all inquiry to scientific inquiry in order to acknowledge and observe this principle of limitation. One need simply acknowledge that, because a man is human in the exercising of his religion and his art, as is the scientist or philosopher, he is limited in vision and understanding to what is available to the human structure, under conditions that influence and shape that structured experience. However much a man may discipline his awareness, or focus his attention, thereby acquiring sensitivity and competence beyond that of the average individual, he is nevertheless conditioned by the limits which human creaturehood lays upon him. In short, the relativity of perspective that conditions scientific inquiry and understanding affects and conditions religious inquiry and understanding as well. And in this sense, the factor of cultural history in any religion looms large, both in the description of its history and in the assessment of its witness of faith. This is not intended as a negative judgment upon any religion. It is a judgment upon the dogmatic and absolute claims of any religion to be the sole bearer of the truth of God, and upon religions that would presume to speak with finality about ultimate aspects of man's nature and destiny without recognizing the cultural and creatural dimensions of its utterances.

It is time that we looked at this issue of absoluteness and cultural relativity in the religions with sober judgment. The fact that one acknowledges the cultural conditioning of any religious faith does not argue that the religion is simply a product of the culture, that its voice is but a pious echo of these cultural sensibilities and mores. To a considerable degree this is precisely what religions tend to be. Yet, with all its cultural conditioning, a religious faith speaks out of depths of ultimacy within and transcending the interplay of cultural activities. It is the nature of the religious response to be an outreach toward realities transcending, judging, and, in some measure, fulfilling these human forms and expectations being shaped within the immediacies of the culture. In religious faiths, therefore, ultimacy and immediacies traffic together. And the religious response is at one and the same time more than a simple echo of a cultural history, yet a genuine participant in the structure of experience that has formed out of the historical events of that culture. No religion is without its hold upon this transcendent outreach, or without a sense of speaking from beyond the common demands and expectations of the cultural experience. And when clergy and priests, as well as theologians, attend to these ultimate aspects to sharpen their focus upon them, they will invariably tend to equate their formulations of a truth apprehended with this absolute measure. In this way, doctrine and theological systems presume to speak with an absolute voice. But this is to bypass or to ignore the principle of limitations which is basic to the human structure, or to any natural structure. What is of ultimate import speaks to and through us, but it does so within the limited purview of the structures of men within any culture. Thus every religion participates in the ultimate dimension of realities, speaks of it, bears witness to it and conveys some measure of its truth among men, but each does so within and through the ambiguous forms and symbols available to its cultural experience. These forms will not body forth in purity and perfection the realities to which they bear witness, though we have instances of a high degree of consonance between God and the Sons of Men in various cultures. Yet it was Jesus who resisted this direct correlation, even with reference to Himself, saying, "Why callest thou me good; there is none good but One, that is God."[3]

Where a proper measure of the cultural forms is taken in any religion, the same kind of humility and tentativeness present among mature scientists in their inquiry is possible. The religious witness is significant for what it is—an offering of the human spirit in response to the ultimate dimension of existence as it has come into the experiences of men within their cultural forms. Variation in cultural forms may mean differences in degrees of men's sensitivity and awareness, differences in the extent or scope to which ultimate realities, with their dimension of sensitivity, can reach the human structure, convey their sensitivities, and shape the cultural experience. To say, therefore, that all religions participate in this ultimate outreach is not to say that all religions are the same, or that they are equal in their response to ultimate demands. The cultural forms both limit and enhance the response to the ultimate structure of sensitivity. And the variation in sensitivity among cultural forms is a significant factor affecting the responses of the religions to what is ultimate in truth and goodness.

The variety in religions thus speaks to many things, among them that cultural experiences have varied; that imagination and human creativity have fashioned different modes of response, celebration, and emulation in the encounter with ultimate demands in experience; that in these responses the human structure has undergone varying degrees of discipline and maturation in its sensitivities and sensibilities, thus conveying through the human psyche, and the cultural mythos, levels of response that are peculiar to its cultural history and shaping.

This variety in religions, I would hold, is not a matter to deplore or to resist. The common notion that there is shame

[3] Matt: 19:17.

or dishonor in the fact that the historic religions differ so widely is a superficial judgment frequently offered by the indifferent observer, or by one generally illiterate in the history of religions. It reflects a lack of understanding both with regard to the nature of religious commitment and with regard to the interplay of religions and the cultures in which their historical development occurs. Given the intensities and ambiguities of every religious response, differences among them are inevitable, and tensions between them are understandable. But differences and tensions are not in themselves evil or expendable. Differences provide variation in the texture of religious faith that bespeaks a depth and quality potential in each of them, but as yet not realized. And tensions can imply a concern with qualitative distinctions in faith, arising from sensitivities in the religious response itself. Wherever the qualitative measure is present, tensions will occur. But tensions may be resolved, while retaining the concern with qualitative distinctions; not by removing the differences, but by religions and cultures learning to live together with their differences, even coming to value these differences for what they afford as further avenues of inquiry.

Much impoverishment in religious understanding has resulted from the timidity of liberated minds in confronting these basic differences among religions. Often, when one has become open enough in one's own religious inquiry to associate with people of other faiths, one feels compelled to suppress all dissonant notions, and to accentuate the bases of agreement, even to the extent of distorting or misrepresenting one's own genuine convictions in the matter. In this way the core of commitments that defines one's own stance, and which has formed out of years of experience and probing, giving integrity to one's own existence and outlook, is relegated to the background, or even disavowed on the assumption that it would be an obstacle to one's association with people of other convictions. One thus becomes hollow and hesitant in one's affirmations, except as one can take up with tenuous, universal judgments that will not offend anyone. In this way the dialogue between people of different faiths becomes vacuous and naïvely utopian, looking to a time when all religions will be one, instead of being seriously explorative and candid in confronting the historic witness of another faith.

The assumption that differences in judgment concerning religious matters must bring offense, or that they will invariably precipitate conflict, overlooks the import and possibilities of disciplined inquiry in religious dialogue. Disciplined inquiry here need not imply the use of a technical discourse, or specialized training for engaging in technical discussion of religious issues. Disciplined religious inquiry need simply imply, on the one hand, a degree of detachment and distance in listening to another witness of faith to enable one to receive what is being offered with a minimum of deflection or obstruction from personal biases and apprehensions, and on the other hand, an affirmation of what has formed as a living conviction in one's own experience with firmness and integrity, but without defensiveness as if resenting or resisting criticism or opposition. A disciplined assertion of affirmations will invite criticism. One cannot avoid feeling distress or even anxiety to some extent in submitting the basic concerns of one's own existence to the judgment of others. And there is always the risk of misunderstanding and false assessment of what one offers. Yet the disciplined person will not only entertain these risks, but will seek to contain the emotional charge that may be evoked by any interchange of thought in this area of intimate beliefs. Even if the containment of intense feeling bearing upon one's own commitment of faith does not altogether succeed, there is value in risking a dialogue in which views are candidly exchanged.[4] I speak here out of experiences in discussing vital issues as a Christian with Hindu and Moslem colleagues. Under some circumstances the venture might prove foolhardy and fruitless, but where it can be undertaken with some measure of confidence and mutual regard such an exchange can be vastly more rewarding than discussions that sidle away from critical issues, preferring to enable its participants to bask in a vacuous mood of goodwill.

You will see from these remarks that my concern in this presentation goes somewhat counter to the emphasis upon achieving one world religion, which is the more common resolution of the problem of religion in an age of science. Let me comment on this point, for it is important to see how the two concerns relate to one another. The zeal to universalize religion, to reach a common denominator in some universal faith is wholly understandable, once one envisages the reality of our common humanity and becomes responsive to horizons of thought made possible in an age of science. And the sensibilities expressed in such a determination are ones that commend themselves to every free and disciplined

[4] There is a growing interest in pursuing this kind of dialogue, despite the problems that are involved. See B. E. Meland, "Theology and the Historian of Religion," *Journal of Religion*, XLI, 4 (October 1961), 263-76; and the chapter on "The Christian Encounter with the Faiths of Men" in *Realities of Faith*. Serious attention is being given to various aspects of this concern by The Christian Institute for the Study of Religion and Society in Bangalore, India. See Paul Devanandan, *Preparation for Dialogue*. Discussions of the problem as it concerns Christians and Hindus appear frequently in the bulletin, *Religion and Society*, published by the Institute under the editorship of M. M. Thomas and Herbert J. Singh. Among Moslem scholars, Isma'il Ragi A. Al Faruqi has given particular attention to this problem of dialogue between Muslims and those of other faiths. See his article, "History of Religions: Its Nature and Significance for Christian Education and the Muslim-Christian Dialogue," *Numen*, XII (January 1965), 35-65. See also Wilfred Cantrell Smith, "Mankind's Religiously Divided History Approaches Self-Consciousness," *Harvard Divinity Bulletin*, October 1964, pp. 1-17, and his *The Meaning and End of Religion*, New York: Macmillan, 1963.

mind. One of the noblest pleas for a universal faith came from the lips of your esteemed countryman, Swami Vivekananda, a generation ago in his memorable appearance at the World Parliament of Religions in Chicago, held in 1893. His vision of faith continues to inspire many Americans still, as was evidenced last year, when two hundred and sixty-seven distinguished American writers and thinkers, along with some of your countrymen, gathered at a dinner to honor his memory on the 100th anniversary of his birth. His vision of faith lives on vigorously in your own country as well, as is evidenced by a moving tribute to him by Professor Suniti Kumar Chatterji, in his essay, "The Basic Unity Underlying the Diversity of Culture" in the book, *Indian Culture*.[5] The lines that speak to our present concern occur in the opening paragraphs, where he is looking beyond Indian culture and beyond all particularistic societies, to the possibility of a single world culture.

With the hope of one world, one mankind and one well-being for all inspiring our men of learning and wisdom to find a path that can be followed by all, this wistful readiness for a single world culture was never greater than now. We leave aside, of course, men of narrow outlook whose intransigent support of one particular pattern is merely an unconscious expression of a blind egotism which has its roots in both ignorance and a desire for domination. The time is indeed ripe, and the stage is set, for a correct understanding of the various patterns of culture and for exploring the methods for their harmonizing, taking our stand on the fundamentals and not on the accidentals, on the agreements and not on the divergence. When this is achieved, and mankind everywhere is trained to accept the fundamental agreement based on the identity of human aspirations, a new chapter in the history of humanity will begin.[6]

[5] Bhikhan Lal Atreya, et al., *Indian Culture*, New Delhi: A Universal Publication.
[6] Ibid. pp. 35-6.

I respond heartily to the vision of these words, and to the sensibility of faith which they convey. Yet, in all candor, I find myself taking issue with what they imply. And in doing so, I hope I do not come under the stricture of Professor Chatterji's censorious reference to "men of narrow outlook whose intransigent support of one particular pattern is merely an unconscious expression of a blind egoism." For I am not concerned to embrace the narrow outlook, or to support with intransigence one particular pattern. I am concerned, however, to do justice to the concrete history and meaning of every religious witness. The historic religions, each in their own way, embody a witness of faith that is distinctive of its opportunity and history, even as it is expressive of its limitations in cultural forms and their attending ambiguities. What is thus conveyed carries hidden treasure of value not only in itself, but to the community of all men who can respond to the attainment of others, or who can encounter the faiths of other men with respect for their history and witness, and with an openness to receive what is given.

This was implied in those famous words uttered by your eminent countryman, Swami Vivekananda, on the occasion to which we have referred. "The Christian is not to become a Hindu or a Buddhist, nor a Hindu or a Buddhist to become a Christian. But each must assimilate the spirit of the others and yet preserve his individuality and grow according to the law of growth."

Once the historic religions can acknowledge the relativity of their cultural forms, even as they make their claims for distinctive disclosures of ultimate reality, they will be prepared not only to engage in self-criticism, but to encounter other faiths with the expectancy and openness that is characteristic of venturers exploring and responding to intimations of the realities evoking their outreach and wonder.

The capacity for self-criticism in any religious tradition is especially important in a scientific age, for without it, the religion must lag before social reforms and creative efforts among the enlightened citizenry of a culture responding to new opportunities for physical and spiritual well-being. Where the principle of limitations is operative in any faith, the devotee can be attentive to distinctions between the realities of its faith, and the cultural expressions of it in any period of its history that have bent the response toward established sensibilities. The faith, however much it may be conveyed through and within such sensibilities and forms, is never identifiable wholly with them; hence a prophetic resistance to such sensibilities, where the vision of experience moves beyond them, may still participate in the witness of faith even as it disavows the cultural expression or form of the faith in any historic period.

Given this acknowledgment of limitation and a capacity for self-criticism in a religion, the encounter between religious faiths can be fruitful and important in a scientific age. Such an encounter, however, would be significant more at the level where intellectual judgments of experience and opinion can be shared than at levels of worship and religious practice. At either level there would be difficulty in transcending or penetrating the barriers of cultural forms, imagery, and symbols that separate the religions; but, in the case of worship and religious practice one would encounter physical barriers as well, where alienating sensibilities and commitments intrude to complicate, if not to preclude, communication or rapport. At the level of intellectual judgments of experience and opinion the clash of symbols and meanings may also be expected, but here there is precedent for abstracting meanings from their concrete context or reference, sufficiently at least to get at general and shared considerations. Or better still, it may be possible for people of disciplined minds of one faith to enter into a more direct and concrete dialogue with comparable people of another faith at the level of what Professor Michael Polyani has called "personal knowledge"—that is, knowledge as it is personally embraced or intended, the knowledge which persons mean as they express it. The more abstract encounter opens up possible areas of collaboration on issues within the culture, enabling people of different faiths to come to judgments upon public issues, and to take their places as fully participating citizens in a secular state. The direct dialogue between persons committed to a particular faith offers opportunity for a negotiation of meaning between persons differing in faith, enabling them to reach not only a level of common humanity, but a concrete encounter of persons as I and Thou in the venture of ultimate concerns.

It is possible that along either path, or in following both simultaneously, the religions of many cultures will achieve a rapport of mutual understanding as well as a rising degree of self-understanding that can provide the ground for seeing the many faiths in some kind of relationship. This, however, remains an abstract and theoretical problem that may or may not serve either the human or the religious situation in any culture. More significantly, however, such encounters and negotiations between peoples of varying faiths increase their awareness of one another as people, as human beings. Somehow in this perception of people as human beings one momentarily breaks through the barrier of cultural forms and symbols to sense the primordial ground of unity that inheres in our humanity. This vision of our universal ground in the Creative Passage that has brought all men into being is a universalism that is genuine, concrete, and actual—not contrived, abstract, or idealized.

Given this vision of an ultimate oneness in our humanity

and a common indebtedness to the Source of our being, many things will follow to mitigate or qualify the erosion of fellow feeling between peoples of different faiths. Conversely much may arise within the thinking and feeling of people to clarify and correlate these differences that divide us.

We come, then, to the conclusion of this 1965 series of the Barrows Lectures. We have sought here to understand the meaning and effect of secularization as it is appearing in the cultures of East and West. It must have become clear to you that my concern has been not only to understand the phenomenon of secularization, but to assess as well the status and import of religious sensibilities in a world becoming increasingly committed to secular ends. Indirectly, I suppose, this poses the question, Is religion receding as secularization advances? Our answer to that question must be that, insofar as religion is equated with static historical forms and sensibilities, we would have to acknowledge that, in certain modern cultures, if not in all, religion so conceived is clearly on the defensive. And the vigor of secularizing forces in modern society would seem to indicate that religion, simply as a social force to perpetuate tradition, will not stand. But amidst the melee of these contemporary forces pressing for the secularization of modern life, there come glimpses of recreative tendencies, offering, yes demanding, a reorientation of the religious vision of life, and, within this new vision of existence and experience, cautioning against the demise of religious sensibilities as such.

Intellectually the problem turns upon the issue of Absoluteness and Relativity. In all spheres of life the principle of limitation is now made to appear foremost, bearing upon the nature of the human structure and thus upon the nature of man, upon the nature of thought, and upon the religious response of men as they encounter depths of reality within their cultural experiences. By a sane recognition of the fact that absoluteness can apply only to the goodness and reality of God as the Ultimate Measure of existence, and that all life within physical and cultural forms participates in the relativity of judgment and understanding, we come at least half way toward breaking through the impasse which continually frustrates our thinking on this issue. But a second step is necessary before we are free to think adequately upon the problem: namely, that, though we participate in the limitations of our cultural forms, and thus partake of their relativity, we participate also, as creatures, in the Ultimacy of the Creative Passage that underlies and carries forward all our humanity; and, in our several ways, we bear witness to this primordial ground of our being. In this we are made more than victims of our illusions, or pawns of our cultural circumstances; for we have access to a perspective upon experience which compels self-criticism and stimulates our encounter with those whose experience differs from our own. And with self-criticism can come self-understanding, which is itself a long step toward understanding other men and the faiths of other men.

There are those in our time who see the resolution of this problem in the creation of a new religion, based upon the intelligent findings of modern man. This view implies the rejection of all historic religions, and the assumption that it is but a matter of time when they will one by one disappear from the face of the earth. I have argued along a different line. The creation of such a new religion, like the nostalgia for an abstract, universal faith, appears to me to be unhistorical, and wholly lacking in an understanding of the concrete character of the religious response. I am appealing to people within the historic faiths who are apprised of the crisis of secularism that is upon us, and who can respond to the religious sensibilities evident among secular minds of our time.

Secularization, wherever and whenever it occurs, is always a threat to historic religions, and, in some instances, it may become a serious social force, dissipating the historical dimension of any culture. It can, however, be quite otherwise; and in some instances, it is being so, injecting into the stream of experience an acidulous ferment that cleanses the inward parts. In the creative ferment that can follow such a purgation and cleansing, I find hope for a resolution of many of our problems. For secularization in modern cultures can then be turned to salutary ends, even to the end of cleansing and reclaiming our religious sensibilities. In so doing, it may direct these sensibilities more realistically to a concern with the Ultimate Realities that inhere in these troubled immediacies—Realities which now stand in judgment of our humanly ambivalent and muddled ways, but which may yet redeem them.

DATE DUE

DE 18 79			
MY 18 72			
MY 27 75			
OC 3 80			
GAYLORD			PRINTED IN U.S A.